NAVIGATING IN TIMES OF CHANGE
The N.E.W.S.® Navigation Journey

Aviad Goz

Dedicated to my beloved Roni that instigated our journey and keeps its flame alive -

Copyright © 2020 Aviad Goz. ALL RIGHTS RESERVED. No part of this publication may be reproduced, stored in a retrieval system, or transmitted in any form or by any means, electronic, mechanical, photocopying, recording, or otherwise without the prior written permission of the publisher and the authors.

Editor: Hedy Caplan

Cover and Layout Design: Diva Moshel

Cover Picture: Nadine Shaabana on Unsplash

Proofread - Sarah Spalding

CONTENTS

PART A – THE DISCOVERY OF THE N.E.W.S.® COMPASS

YOUR STARTING POINT	9
THE MAP	11
THE LANDSCAPE OF YOUR JOURNEY	16
CONSTANT CHANGE AND THE IMPACT ON PEOPLE AND ORGANIZATIONS	18
YOUR JOURNEY OF NAVIGATION	21
MY PHILOSOPHY FOR NAVIGATION	23

PART B – NAVIGATING WITH THE N.E.W.S.® COMPASS

THE N.E.W.S.® NORTH INTRODUCTION	26
YOUR PERSONAL JOURNEY IN THE NORTH	31
YOUR SECOND STEP IN THE PERSONAL JOURNEY IN THE NORTH	40
YOUR NEXT VERSION	46
STEP THREE IN THE PERSONAL JOURNEY IN THE NORTH - PRACTICAL VISION	54
ONE STEP DEEPER INTO THE PERSONAL NORTH	57
THE N.E.W.S.® PERSONAL JOURNEY IN THE EAST - INTRODUCTION	59
THE PERSONAL JOURNEY IN THE EAST	62
THE FIRST STEP IN YOUR PERSONAL EAST JOURNEY	66
SECOND STEP IN YOUR PERSONAL JOURNEY IN THE EAST	70
THIRD STEP IN YOUR PERSONAL JOURNEY IN THE EAST – TRANSLATE YOUR VALUES INTO BEHAVIORS.	73
PERSONAL EAST - ONE STEP DEEPER	75
THE N.E.W.S.® PERSONAL JOURNEY IN THE SOUTH	76
THE PERSONAL JOURNEY IN THE SOUTH - INTRODUCTION	82
FIRST STEP IN THE PERSONAL JOURNEY IN THE SOUTH – IDENTIFY YOUR LIMITING BELIEFS	84
STEP ONE IN YOUR PERSONAL JOURNEY IN THE SOUTH IDENTIFYING YOUR LIMITING BELIEFS	87
STEP TWO IN THE PERSONAL SOUTH JOURNEY: MAKE YOUR CHOICE.	95
STEP THREE IN PERSONAL SOUTH JOURNEY - BREAK THROUGH YOUR LIMITS	98
PERSONAL SOUTH - ONE STEP DEEPER	104
YOUR PERSONAL JOURNEY IN THE WEST	106
YOUR PERSONAL JOURNEY IN THE WEST INTRODUCTION	109
FIRST STEP IN THE PERSONAL WEST -DEFINING CRITICAL YEARLY GOALS	111
SECOND STEP IN THE PERSONAL WEST - CREATE YOUR TACTICAL PLAN	113
THIRD STEP IN THE PERSONAL WEST- SET A "WEEKLY FOCUS"	114
PERSONAL WEST - ONE STEP DEEPER	116

PART C - YOUR N.E.W.S.® LEADERSHIP JOURNEY

INTRODUCTION	119
THE FIRST STEP OF YOUR LEADERSHIP PRE- NAVIGATION	133
THE SECOND STEP OF YOUR LEADERSHIP PRE- NAVIGATION	135
EARTHQUAKE - THE UNAVOIDABLE	137
TRANSITION FROM ORGANIZATIONS BASED ON SURVIVAL AND CONTROL TO ORGANIZATIONS BASED ON PERSONAL GREATNESS	137
YOUR LEADERSHIP JOURNEY IN THE NORTH	141
INTRODUCTION TO YOUR LEADERSHIP JOURNEY IN THE NORTH	145
CREATE YOUR TEAM'S PRACTICAL STRATEGY	155
CREATE AND ENGAGE YOUR TEAM WITH A PRACTICAL VISION	158
WHERE IS MY ORGANIZATION GOING?	162
YOUR LEADERSHIP JOURNEY IN THE EAST	166
YOUR LEADERSHIP JOURNEY IN THE EAST - INTRODUCTION	169
THE FIRST STEP IN YOUR LEADERSHIP JOURNEY IN THE EAST – DISCOVERING COMMON IMPORTANCE	173
THE SECOND STEP OF YOUR LEADERSHIP JOURNEY IN THE EAST	174
THE THIRD STEP IN YOUR LEADERSHIP JOURNEY IN THE EAST	176
THE MEANING REVOLUTION	177
YOUR LEADERSHIP JOURNEY IN THE SOUTH	179
SOUTH LEADERSHIP JOURNEY - INTRODUCTION	181
THE FIRST STEP IN YOUR LEADERSHIP JOURNEY IN THE SOUTH: THE LIMITING STORY	182
THE SECOND STEP IN YOUR LEADERSHIP JOURNEY IN THE SOUTH: THE EMPOWERING STORY	184
YOUR THIRD STEP IN THE LEADERSHIP JOURNEY IN THE SOUTH – BREAK THROUGH THE LIMITS	186
YOUR LEADERSHIP JOURNEY IN THE WEST	188
YOUR LEADERSHIP JOURNEY IN THE WEST - INTRODUCTION	191
STEP ONE IN YOUR LEADERSHIP JOURNEY IN THE WEST – CRITICAL GOALS	194
STEP TWO IN YOUR LEADERSHIP JOURNEY IN THE WEST – TACTICAL PLANS	197
STEP THREE IN YOUR LEADERSHIP JOURNEY IN THE WEST – WEEKLY FOCUS AND FOLLOW-UP	200
CONCLUSION	202

PART D - OUR N.E.W.S.® JOURNEY

INTRODUCTION	203
GLOBAL EXPANSION AND NETWORK	207
SPECIAL PROJECTS	211
CULTURES AND THE N.E.W.S.® COMPASS	218
POSITIONING	220
RESEARCH	223
THE FUTURE	225
OUR PARTNERS	226
CONCLUSION	237

Welcome.

I would like to invite you to a journey that will change your life, your career and your organization, as it has changed mine.

Following extensive research, conducted for over 20 years with thousands of people and hundreds of organizations, I discovered the N.E.W.S.® Compass.

I have always been deeply interested in how individuals, teams and organizations get "stuck" on their way to fulfilling their potential.

Most research and books focus on the few successful ones. But I was more concerned about those that didn't make it.

I found four core reasons why most do not fulfill their potential. This finding led to the creation of the N.E.W.S.® Compass.

Since then, the compass has proven to be a most effective tool for navigating in times of change.

Millions have used it around the globe, including start-ups and Fortune 100 companies in 5 continents and more than 40 countries. It has changed the lives of many and led individuals, teams and organizations to experience success.

I would like to invite you to begin this journey for yourself.

You might be a university student wondering which professional direction to take, a business owner or manager concerned about the next phase for yourself and your organization in a constantly changing world, or an individual at a crossroad in your life or career, wondering how best to navigate yourself and how to make the best choices. You might be a leader wanting to lead your team more effectively. For all of you, the N.E.W.S.® Compass and its different applications will be a very powerful and useful tool.

So, let's take this journey together - a journey that starts inside of you and then expresses itself in the world.

Do not worry. When you return the cat will still be napping on the sofa. The kettle will still be warm. You, however, will be transformed into the next best version of yourself, ready to lead the next phase of your life, your career or your leadership journey.

PART A – THE DISCOVERY OF THE N.E.W.S.® COMPASS

For you
Before starting our transformational journey, let me share with you how the N.E.W.S.® Compass was discovered. This will give you a broader perspective for understanding the journey you are about to experience. This is the story of the last 64 years of my life. I invite you to write your story alongside mine.

Early beginnings
"Grant us the time to see our whisper turn into the roar of the crowd" R.A.

Since childhood, I have constantly been interested in creating alternative solutions to complex problems, starting with mathematics in the second grade of elementary school. Every subject I studied has stimulated me to look for alternative answers and solutions from math to social problems and economical complexities, from biology and science to religions.

I became particularly interested in personal and organizational development. The drive to find better solutions for individuals, teams and organizations drove me to navigate my career in the direction of developing people and organizations. I chose to become a trainer, coach and facilitator for multinational companies around the world and have helped many individuals and organizations improve their effectiveness, sales and culture.

I have been consistently scouting unfulfilled potential and helping people translate this potential pragmatically in their lives and their work.

In my twenties, I studied science, psychology, religions and ancient cultures. I was interested primarily in personal development, as a result, I set up personal development groups and trained many young people. In my thirties, I moved into training people how to communicate effectively and present their ideas or products. So, sales, marketing and presentation skills became my area of focus.

In my forties, I moved into personal and interpersonal effectiveness. I liaised with Steven Covey and delivered hundreds of programs around the globe, covering 7 Habits of Effectiveness, time management and leadership skills.

It was then that I realized that I have a ten-year cycle, and at the end of every ten years, I move on to the next subject. I have since realized that most people have cycles, some shorter, some longer. They may not even be aware of them but will feel compelled to move on at the end of a precise period of time.

I have consistently felt compelled to create new solutions, new approaches, new models, new mindsets, new tools, and have accompanied thousands of executives and teams in more than 2,000 organizations in 50 countries. I created training companies and trained many others to help individuals and organizations on their path to development.

In my fifties, I became intensely interested in understanding why individuals, teams and organizations get stuck on their way to reaching their full potential. I realized that most research was focused on the few successful individuals and companies "that made it". Books such as "Built to Last", "Good to Great", "In Search of Excellence", "Seven Habits of Highly Effective People" and more, were great inspiration.

But I wanted to understand why the other 95% of people and organizations do not become "Great". Why did they get "stuck" on their way to success? There was very little research or literature on this question.

So, true to my need to create new solutions, I set upon the path of unlocking this enigma and finding ways to improve upon it.

Over a period of years, I conducted research with HR and Organizational Development professionals, managers and leaders of organizations.

The more I learned, the more I realized with great surprise that the reasons for getting stuck on the way to greatness and fulfilment were similar for individuals, teams and entire organizations. This was a revelation that a universal principle was at play. The evidence showed me clearly that the root causes for getting stuck can be divided into four main categories:

1. Being unclear about the future - Not knowing the next step, losing sight of the direction for the future. Lacking a vision.
2. Suffering a lack of motivation or engagement - Losing the drive, the motivation and the energy to persevere.
3. Having internal barriers –limitations, limiting beliefs about what might be possible and settling into comfort zones, complaining and becoming a "Victim".
4. Having issues with planning and execution – Having problems with ordered planning and disciplined execution necessary to achieve desired goals.

These four areas seem to cover a multitude of reasons why people, teams, and organizations get "stuck" on their way.

The analogy of driving a car might make this clearer.

A driver might not reach their destination for several reasons. Firstly, the driver might not know where they are going. Secondly, there is no fuel in the tank. Thirdly, they are driving with the handbrake on, and fourthly, they have no map or GPS to chart their path. It is no wonder that any of these reasons could stop a person, a team or an organization from advancing effectively.

I was not yet sure what to do with this realization of the four main reasons for getting "stuck" and kept thinking and researching until one day I took a hot bath.

This is not a story. Welcome to my reality. From a young age I have found that I create best in a hot water environment.

Here is a thought for you:

For you
Do you, the reader, know the environment in which you think or create best? Is it in the open air? Is it with your feet on the ground in nature? Is it near rolling streams? At the seaside?

Great artists have always found their inspiring environments, from the special light in Southern France for Van Gogh to the wild nature near a lake for Ralph Waldo Emerson.

I believe we owe it to ourselves to be aware of the environments that are the most inspiring and productive for us, and to go there as often as possible.

So, my element is hot water. It could be a warm sea.

I wrote my first book in 24 hours at the Red Sea. It could be a jacuzzi, where I wrote some other books. Or hot springs, where I wrote many articles. And it could even be a hot bath.

It is not very practical to write in those environments but there are solutions for everything!

So, that particular day I turned to a hot bath with the intention of "cracking" this issue of the four groupings of reasons for getting "stuck". I wanted to make something useful out of it.

After soaking in the hot water for a while, I had a "flash". Out of nowhere came the idea that these four groupings together could form a compass with four directions.

Each direction could represent one of the areas of being "stuck" and the type of solution needed to overcome that situation. I could actually see a compass in my imagination. It appeared as an organizing model.

It was so very clear, and I knew instantly that:

The North will answer the question: "Where do we go from here?"

Getting "stuck" in the North is not being able to answer this question with complete clarity and lucidity.

The East will answer the question: "Why do we want to go there and what will drive it?"

Getting "stuck" in the East is not being able to answer this question with conviction.

The South will answer the question: "Why not?" What stops us from getting to our North?

Getting "stuck" in the South is not being able to overcome these obstacles with courage and resolution.

The West will answer the question: "How to get there?" How to plan? How to execute our intentions effectively?

Getting "stuck" in the West is not being able to answer this question with determination and precision.

It was astonishing in its simplicity.

I then saw the colors of each direction.

The North would be Red like a well-focused ruby laser beam, symbolizing singularity of intention regarding the future.

The East would be Yellow like the color of the sun that provides energy and life, symbolizing motivation and drive.

The West would be Blue, the color of law and order in many cultures, symbolizing the order and discipline of planning and execution.

Here came to mind the old Latin saying "Ex oriente lux, ex occidente Lex" "From the East comes the light, from the West come law and order".

The ancient Romans observed that cultures from the East were more concerned with enlightenment and cultures from the West with law and order.

Interestingly, this ancient observation still has some relevance today as well.

So, the East will be light and energy, and the West will be ordered planning and execution.

The South would be Green which symbolizes growth beyond limitations and barriers.

I realized that this compass could help people and organizations to understand where they are "Stuck" and what to do about it.

It would allow them to navigate beyond limitations and liberate movement toward their North.

I decided that the most appropriate name for it would be the N.E.W.S.® Compass, an abbreviation of North, East, West and South.

I had the feeling of "Eureka" like Archimedes in his ancient bath in his time. This revelation, this insight and its details that followed my extensive research were astonishing and exhilarating. I was really deeply moved, as if I had touched some universal understanding and wisdom.

Yet I did not know what to do in practical terms with this N.E.W.S.® compass, its meanings and colors that appeared so complete and so clear.

Sometime later, I was lecturing on personal effectiveness at a large conference center. After the lecture a few people approached me to ask further questions. Amongst them was my wife to be – Roni. She asked if I could share with her some deeper knowledge about personal development and its principles in the universe.

I was surprised and when I asked her why she would ask me such a question, she answered in her wise way "I knew that you would know".

I then had a very strong feeling that the newly discovered compass could help me answer her enquiry.

I set up a meeting with her to tell her about the four directions of being "stuck" and the four directions of development.

Roni was fascinated and asked if she could hear more about this compass and the four directions of becoming "unstuck".

The first meeting was outstanding and more followed. That journey evolved into two years and roughly 60 coaching sessions, all dedicated to her personal development journey based on the N.E.W.S.® Compass.

Her amazing journey of development was inspiring and at the end of the two years, we wondered how to share with others this amazingly effective compass that had turned out to be a systematic coaching method for personal development.

Eventually we agreed that each of us would coach two people free of charge using the N.E.W.S.® Compass on the condition that they would each in turn coach two more people for free, as well. The idea was to share this knowledge and practice and develop it as a goodwill gift to people, especially those who were at a point where they needed to navigate their life and career.

Soon we had more than 40 people coaching each other with the compass; and a small, dedicated community of practitioners came into being.

At this stage, the N.E.W.S.® compass was used for a two-year navigation journey of personal development and was intended solely for a pro bono sharing and gifting amongst friends and colleagues.

As the use of the compass expanded, Roni came up with the idea that we could train coaches to use the N.E.W.S.® Compass in a more complete way.

This was in 2003, and it was the birth of what would become the N.E.W.S.® Global expansion.

At this stage I would like to share the N.E.W.S.® Compass with you, the reader. It appears very simple at first, but its application is vast and profound.

The N.E.W.S.® Compass

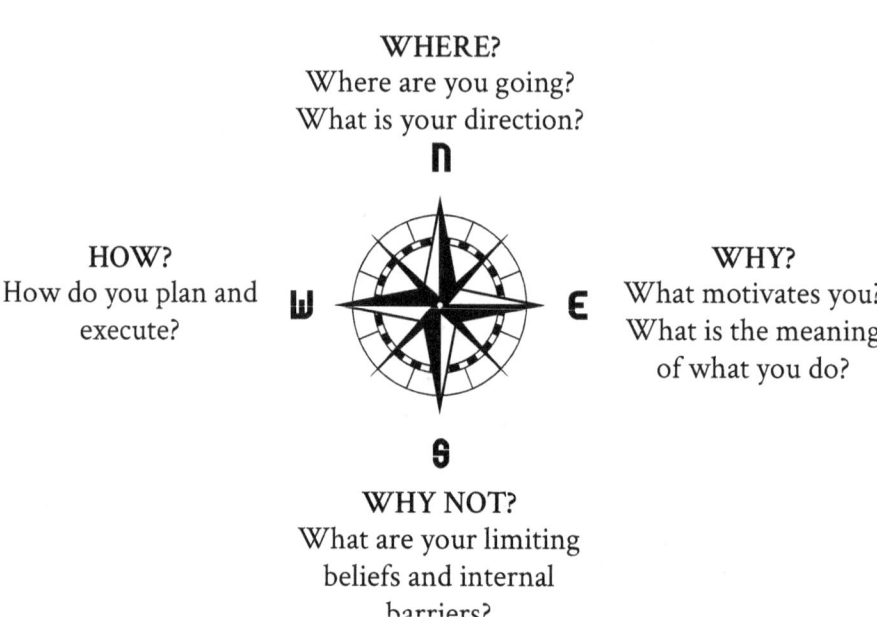

WHERE?
Where are you going?
What is your direction?

HOW?
How do you plan and execute?

WHY?
What motivates you?
What is the meaning of what you do?

WHY NOT?
What are your limiting beliefs and internal barriers?

Each direction represents a specific type of blockage. It can be defined by specific questions. Each direction focuses on a particular set of solutions and a domain of development.

YOUR STARTING POINT

For you
Here are some foundations for your personal journey with the N.E.W.S.® Compass.

"To embark on a journey without knowing the starting point is to get lost."
Aviad Goz

Humans are conscious intelligent beings. That makes us totally unique on this planet and even beyond. One of the best definitions of intelligence is "Knowing exactly one's situation at any given time".

This is often easier said than done.

We all dip our toes in the vast ocean of the universe, trying to understand our place in it. Each creating our different realities from that understanding.

Every journey has a point of departure. What is yours? How do you assess it?

We do not always know where we're going, but we need to know at least where we are starting from.

Often we believe we are in a different place then we actually are. This leads people and organizations, alike, to proceed from erroneous assumptions and mistakes.

If you have ever navigated with a map before GPS or Google maps were invented, you probably remember how challenging it can be to determine your location. You always need some external references to assess where you are.

Your starting point is a crossroad. From this crossroad there are endless paths leading to different directions. The crossroad can be a result of some external situation like a new job offer or simply frustration with your current job.

A crossroad can also be created just by pausing and deciding to review your situation. Every pause, every review can actually create a crossroad from which there are endless ways to continue in the field of all possibilities.

To understand your position at a crossroad, you need some external viewpoint. You need to zoom out to an elevated point to see the larger context of it all.

It is like taking off in a helicopter and viewing the situation from above.

When you are inside a situation, with the personal and emotional involvement, you do not see much.

THE MAP

Most people view their location in life in relation to family or career, these most common external references.

"I have been stuck with this terrible boss for three years already", or "I am in a really good relationship with my kids."

If you elevate your point of view a bit, you might see the neighborhood or group of friends that will give you a different assessment of your location. "I am very active in the neighborhood commitee." Some people will view their organizational landscape as the map with which they navigate. If you go even higher you might see the nation or country in which you live, for which you sometimes are ready to go to battle and sacrifice lives, yours, or others'. Some other times your national belonging will lead you to just cheer for your national team at an international football match.

It is the context that defines your journey and your location or positioning in it.

If you go even higher you might perceive humanity and the time in which you live and your role in it. And even higher still you can perceive the planet, its needs and current challenges, and wonder what you can do in this larger context.

And, of course, you can perceive the entire universe and your role or contribution in it.

Each viewpoint creates the arena or the map in which you consciously live and operate.

A person can spend their entire life in the family arena and identify totally with it.

Or live and operate in a much larger arena that provides a totally different sense of meaning to what they do.

This is not a metaphor or an analogy. Different people operate in different arenas and navigate with different maps.

In each arena a person creates their version of reality and what is most important for them.

"Human consciousness that has expanded can never shrink back to where it was before" says the wise man.

In this journey of yours you have to decide which map you will use. What is the larger context that matters the most to you?

Note: The higher your viewpoint, the more you will see things and people as unified. The lower your viewpoint, you will see more what is different between people and things.

"The map is not the territory" says the wise man.

For you
Please decide now which map you will use for your journey.
Is it your career? your organization? your relationships? your role and contribution?
Therefore, the crossroad you are at can be a family crossroad, a career crossroad, a major life crossroad, a meaning crossroad or any other.

Being at a crossroad is not necessarily easy or comfortable. There are different options. There are many voices and ways of reasoning. It can be confusing.

People may spend years at a crossroad procrastinating before choosing their path, weighing the different options and reasoning endlessly, blended with emotion and uncertainty.

When you do not have a clear compass, decisions can become challenging. "What will I study? What my parents want or what my friends are doing?" "Shall I leave this secured well-paying job and start my own dream business?"

"Shall we develop the product with the new technology or stick to what we already know so well?"

"Will I champion this organizational development? Or leave it to others?"

Crossroads challenge us. These days with rapid changes all around, we may find ourselves at crossroads most of the time. Choice was never so available for so many people. Choice is a blessing and can be a curse when it becomes confusing. Your journey is from one crossroad to the next.

At crossroads you exercise choice and by that choice, create the next chapter of your journey, your career, your life.

In this book we will explore two maps:
1. Your personal journey map.
2. Your leadership journey map.

The personal arena is of utmost importance for most people.

The leadership, team or business arena is where people spend most of their awake time.

It impacts them greatly in many ways.

In the leadership arena, I will address people who choose to be leaders and managers either of themselves or others.

For you
To assess your position, I would like to offer you a brief version of the N.E.W.S.® assessment to help you locate your starting point easily.

Personal Characterization Short Assessment
On a scale of 1 – 5, to what degree does each one of the following sentences apply to your situation on your "map" today?

1 – Definitely incorrect, 2 – Partially incorrect, 3 – Partially correct, 4 – Quite correct, 5 – Definitely correct

NORTH
1. I have a clear direction for my development in this area.

2. I have long-term goals for the next 3- 5 years in this area.

3. My goals are written down and used as a working tool.
Total _____

EAST

1. I have a clear set of values that guide me in this area.
2. I live according to my values in my daily life and work.
3. I am passionate and excited about this area.
Total _____

WEST
1. I have a clear working plan to achieve my goals in this area.
2. I follow a clear schedule to achieve these goals.
3. I plan and execute each and every week based on my goals.
Total _____

SOUTH
1. I feel I am constantly improving and developing in this area.
2. I renew myself and feel more and more empowered.
3. I intentionally step out of my comfort zone and seek new challenges in this area.
Total _____

For you
Analyze your results.
If in any of the directions, you scored:
13 and above, your situation in that direction is positive and progressive.
9-12, your situation in that direction is average. There is some work to be done to progress and develop.
Below 9, you may currently be "stuck" in that direction. You could benefit from using the different tools that will be shared later in this book.

Let me share some examples that might explain your results better.

If you have a strong North and weak East, it means that you know where you want to go, but you currently lack the drive or motivation to do so.

If your East is strong and your West is weak, it might mean that you are highly energized and driven but lack the ability to translate your drive and passion into a concrete plan with tangible results.

If your North is strong and your South is weak, it means that you know what you want, but you are burdened by fears and hesitations and therefore cannot really move forward.

If your South is strong and your North is weak, you are a courageous person who breaks through limits as a way of life, but currently you have no idea where you want to move on to.

Here you will find a more concise version of the fuller assessment, so you get a feel for the importance of starting with clarity as to where you are currently.

www.newsnavigation.com

For you
This was the N.E.W.S.® Compass assessment on a small scale to allow you to assess your current position on the map that you have chosen. Now, let's explore what it was designed for – Navigating in Times of Change.

THE LANDSCAPE OF YOUR JOURNEY

For you
When you go on a journey the terrain and the landscape have great importance and can make for an easy journey like "walking in the park" or a challenging hike, like mountaineering in rough terrain.

Times of change
"Change has become the new constant." Aviad Goz

We live in a time that has no precedence in human history, which professionals call VUCA time. This acronym stands for Volatility, Uncertainty, Complexity and Ambiguity, a term brought to business in the last decade to describe the volatile, uncertain situation of markets and economies. As is true for so many other terms, the term VUCA is taken from the military and describes a situation in the middle of battle when the chaos is so extreme that no one knows anymore what is really going on. Are we winning or losing? Are those forces ours or the enemy? VUCA is a state in the midst of the dust and heat of the battle, the wounded cries and the madness that rages around.

We live in a time of volatility, where markets, economies and social and political orders move up and down like an unpredictable roller coaster. The uncertainty of what tomorrow will bring is a major factor. The questions are many:

Which technology will take over? What will tomorrow's career opportunities be? What will the next political turmoil be?

Our daily work and lives are much more complex and demanding than those of our parents. We try to accomplish so much in our over-crowded days, juggling unlimited accessibility and endless quantities of information to process. Ambiguity rules. No one fully understands the trends of the global economy, the waves of refugees, health concerns, the messages of politicians. You would have to be a historian, a tech expert, an economist, a futurist and a sociologist all at the same time to begin to grasp just how much of the current situation you do not really understand.

The world is changing at a rapid rate with forces radically reshaping the reality in which we live. At the start of the 21st century, Ray Kurzweil, futurist and chief engineer at Google, predicted that 20,000 years of progress would be crammed into the next 100 years.

While the world has always experienced change, the rate of change is accelerating. Markets, business models and technologies are transforming at a pace unlike anything past generations have ever witnessed. From global warming to financial crises, shifting social and demographic trends, resource scarcity, living inside social media, excessive availability and an onslaught of new addictions, diseases and plagues. Everywhere we look disruptive innovations are impacting every sector, generating high levels of turmoil.

No company, industry or individual career is immune to the impact of these forces.

We are amidst global climate change we ourselves have caused. Some deny it and many disregard our responsibility to do something about it, if indeed we still can.

Change as a constant is radically reshaping the way we live, work, survive and thrive. And at the same time, we still crave security and safety. We crave for things to stay as we were promised.

We want equal opportunity for all, a fair distribution of wealth, upgrades in our situation in our lifetime.

At the root of these changes are technological advances that have occurred at a breathtaking speed. Many are overwhelmed and no longer able to cope, while others hope for things to return to "normal". Those of us who have undergone any major upheaval or change may still shy away from embracing change as a way of life, mostly because we lack the tools, skills and mindset to deal with it effectively.

As people living in a world substantially more volatile, uncertain and complex, incremental changes are no longer sufficient. Frequent and deeper changes and transformation are needed.

CONSTANT CHANGE AND THE IMPACT ON PEOPLE AND ORGANIZATIONS

This period of accelerating change has put a strain on individuals, organizations and entire societies. Global trends are hitting faster, harder, and broader, with results that can be both exhilarating and devastating for individuals, companies, industries and entire regions. In 1970, the futurist Alvin Toffler predicted that people exposed to such rapid changes of modern life would suffer from shattering stress and disorientation. They would be, in his words, "future-shocked". The intensifying problems of uncertainty and anxiety resulting from too much change lead to feelings of helplessness, despair, uncertainty, insecurity, anxiety and burnout. Most people can handle a certain amount of change, and feel they know how to deal with it, albeit reactively. However, the problem today is that we are overloaded with more change than we can adapt to or handle.

The fast rate of change in the world today is impacting organizations everywhere and therefore their people. Globalization is rapidly redefining today's business environment and many well-managed companies like RIM, Nokia, Barnes & Noble, B&O, Kodak and Blockbuster have been disrupted by rapidly shifting technologies. Others are challenged by new business models based on collaborative consumption (books/media, car sharing, home sharing, parking). A high degree of customer loyalty is a thing of the distant past.

Today's organizations are all struggling with the reality of change, which often threatens their very survival. Learning to cope with change is a key management and leadership skill for this era. Navigating through change successfully and helping others to participate actively has become essential.

Your Journey of Navigation

For you
To conduct a journey in a changing environment you need to navigate.

It is no longer sufficient to have a vision for 10 years from now, draw a straight line and hope that it will come true.

As you move, you need to continually refer to the map. You need to reassess the changes in you and around you. You need to set a long-term perspective and simultaneously stay focused on the pragmatic aspects of the very short-term, including adaptability.

But the truth is that you have been navigating all your life. This is what has brought you thus far.

Where choice and navigation are concerned there are three stages in life:

Birth to puberty – This is a time when you are not yet fully responsible for your choices and therefore for your navigation. It is still mainly in the hands of parents, teachers and mentors. Although even that is becoming more and more fragile.

Puberty to maturity – This is the time of the great navigation. You set to the sea of life and every choice you make defines your journey. You are fully responsible for navigating between crossroads and the fruit of our navigation is the life and career that you create.

Old age – This period has no defined age but is rather a mentality. It is signified by giving up on navigating and becoming fixed and set in habits and ways of functioning. For some this stage might happen early in life, and for others it maay never arrive. This is the stage when we become the sweet or sour fruit of our lifelong navigation.

For you
It is clear that if you are reading this book you have navigated your life to this point.

Let me share with you a great tool I have created that might give you some important insights about your navigation thus far.

Think about the major decisions you have made in your life: What to study?

Where to live?

The first step in a career? Professional transitions, etc.

Go back in your memory to all these crossroads.

For each, try to remember the reasons for each decision at the time. Was it a need for security or the need for challenge?

Was it social pressure or the drive for freedom? Was it financially driven? Or propelled by comfort? Or maybe by your parents? Or was it simply the most interesting option available?

Go through these crossroads one by one and recall the decision-making code you used at the time.

Do you see any patterns? Is there a sequence? Similarities? Do you observe the same code, or did it change at some point?

Doing this exercise candidly will reveal your hidden compass for navigation. It will reveal how you have navigated thus far.

Was it conscious? That is doubtful. Was it by choice? That is questionable.

Now you are at the point where you can choose freely if you keep this compass for life or change it for the kind of compass I will offer in this book:

The compass of your Greatness.

YOUR JOURNEY OF NAVIGATION

Navigation means creating and leading the next phase for yourself, your family or group, your team and/or your business or organization.

The development of navigation through history is fascinating: from stellar navigation to compasses, gyroscopes and, finally, GPS systems. The modern GPS simplifies the navigation process so the user can forge ahead confidently through unfamiliar territory toward new destinations. In the past, many ships, caravans and travelers lost their way due to poor navigation.

Navigating yourself, your team and your organization in a sea of uncertainty and ambiguity is a complex task. It requires identifying the starting point, and the current and future trends in the environment.

All families, societies, teams and organizations must have navigators. They can be patriarchs or matriarchs in the family. Elected leaders or dictators. A board of directors, senior management or a general manager in organizations. It is interesting to note that organizations have boards of directors, a term that is derived from the word "direction".

Navigation involves constantly creating the next phase or chapter in an evolving, ever-changing scenario in order to reach an end goal or a vision. A word that is often used in navigating teams, societies or organizations is – Strategy.

Strategy, a military term, is derived from the Greek word "Strategos" – an army leader, and the word – "Strata" which means – plain.

In ancient times, the only way to command a battle was to stand at an elevated place to have a bird's eye view of the entire battlefield below.

From this "overview" leaders could reach major decisions about the battle. Strategy, following the historic example, means the ability to make major decisions based on a broad perspective or point of view.

Over the last 25 years, however, many have found that setting a strategy, vision and mission is only a very small part of what is actually required to navigate. The present economic and social conditions, the complexity of markets, competition, and frequent and radical changes make it almost impossible to navigate oneself, much less an organization, seamlessly.

Just 15 years ago many organizations could set a vision for the next 7- 10 years. People had a lifelong vision.

Today, it would be futile for organizations or individuals to attempt anything definitive with such a long timeframe, because of the constant interruptions caused by the volatility of the economic environment, which will simply impede and slow down the process.

In the book "Built to Last", published in 1994, the authors Collins & Porras described 16 companies that held the position of market leaders for more than a hundred years and were "built to last".

Now, 24 years later, 12 of those companies no longer exist. The other four have lost their market leadership. This indicates the degree of change as well as the acute need to "read the map" to navigate effectively. In the last decade, there are many famous examples of companies that did not navigate well and lost their market share or were sold, including Nokia, Kodak and Blackberry, to name just a few. Millions of other small and large companies were wiped out of existence because they were not able to "read the map" well, or they took "wrong turns" in their navigation process.

Navigation requires constant and conscious engagement. Autopilot will not work here. Hands-on, real-time navigation is necessary in environments of constant change and ambiguity.

Decisions about careers, future plans, policies, products, development, recruiting etc., are all acts of navigation that influence the course, for each one of us and for organizations alike.

To navigate well, one needs a compass, a GPS, or some other system that can be trusted and used easily by individuals, teams and organizations. This system must respond to and address the many complexities inside and outside the life of an individual, a family, society, and the progression of organizations.

To navigate effectively in times of change requires a clear philosophy and principles.

MY PHILOSOPHY FOR NAVIGATION

"If the wind in your sails is strong enough, you can travel any distance."
Aviad Goz

There are profound reasons why we do what we do in the world.

The N.E.W.S.® journey and global impact stems from our authentic calling and inner voice as to what people and organizations need at this time of change.

At the start of the global expansion and deployment of N.E.W.S.®, we were very clear that our work with individuals and organizations would be aligned with the set of principles we believe in.

Principles remain constant despite chaos and entropy.

They determine what works and what does not work and are like the grains around which reality unfolds and develops.

They are beyond personal preferences and are true and universal, like structures of intelligence that make things work the way they do.

In my search for the underlying, inviolable principles of effective self-transformation, I talked to thousands of people in many countries and hundreds of organizations. I heard their stories and analyzed them. I tried to connect the dots and understand the patterns and repeated evidence of these principles.

I chose principles that would guide our work with individuals and organizations and would emphasize the human aspect and help people thrive and develop.

I knew very well that most societies and organizations were mainly focused on profit, power and the bottom line, and yet we decided to drive our philosophy as a balancing factor.

My approach has always been to foster the interconnectedness of individual potential and fulfillment, and society or organizational needs.

Following are our principles for the personal journey:

- Creating your own life and career – Each individual is responsible for creating their life and career inside the circumstances within which they find themselves. They are in the driver's seat. There is no one else to blame or hold responsible.
- Navigation – Each individual can create the next chapter in their journey towards fulfillment and greatness. The way people Navigate occurs through their decisions and movements at crossroads all along the way.
- Choice – Navigation happens though choice. Choice is a unique given human endowment. It is the birthright and responsibility of each individual to exercise conscious free choice to guide their journey. By our choices we create our journey from one crossroad to the next.
- Compass – When navigating and making choices, individuals use a decision-making code to make their choices at crossroads. It can be a chosen conscious and reasoning code or by default, a habitual one. The most authentic decision-making compass is the one navigates to your Greatness and potential.
- Greatness - Each person's innate, unique, and authentic potential and contribution. We encourage people to use it as their compass for self-navigation.
- Inside – Out – Individuals can use an approach of navigating their journey according to their true passions and core capabilities rather than through and opportunistic outside-in approach.

For working with teams and organizations

For leadership development training, we expanded our principles. Those principles cover the area of people who work together.

- Participative leadership – We live in a time and age that requires a new type of leadership that is more participative, rather the historic "Top – down" style of the industrial era. This is because the world of work is evolving to "knowledge age" workers and Millennials. This type of employee needs to be involved, to understand and to have influence, and they are looking to develop this in the workplace.

- Creating together – For teams to be engaged and aligned, they need to create their joint N.E.W.S.® compass together. When they create it together, they own it and are accountable for it. The global lack of engagement is mainly due to the top- down, directive approach which leads to a lack of involvement of people in deciding together where they are headed.
- Joint alignment – For the alignment of teams and the organization as a whole, people need to understand where the organization is going and work out their derivative targeting accordingly with their managers and leaders.
- Leadership – Leadership starts with self- leadership. From this, it can expand to leadership of others and only then to leadership of teams. Leadership is the act of directing, engaging and inspiring people to move from where they are to where they can be. Leadership is a choice, not just a one-time choice, but on an ongoing basis. Management can be learned. Leadership must be chosen again and again!
- Organizations based on Greatness – Contemporary organizations are based on the talents of their people and not on fear and control. This is a line of evolution that companies are slowly moving into at varying speeds and to different degrees.

All our work with individuals, teams and organizations globally is based on these principles. As the years go by and we have organizations that have worked with us for 5 or 6 years and even 12 years in some cases, we realize that we have actually changed the way people work together and made it more participative, collaborative and aligned. We see that we help create great organizations both in their culture and D.N.A and in their business results.

This realization provides a deep assurance that what we do has emerged beyond proof of concept into actual global impact.

For you
We invite you, the reader, to take the N.E.W.S.® journey with us. You can take the personal journey as an individual. You can also choose to take the leadership journey if it suits your needs or interests.

PART B – NAVIGATING WITH THE N.E.W.S.® COMPASS

For you
Let's begin a great journey. This journey can be a personal journey or as a team manager or leader of an organization.

These two journeys and the interconnectedness between them will be the backbone of this book. The individual journey can apply to all.

The leadership journey is for leaders or managers or those who wish to lead others in these times of change.

THE N.E.W.S.® NORTH INTRODUCTION

North sayings

"If one does not know to which port one is sailing, no wind is favorable."

Seneca

"If you do not know where you are going, you will probably end up somewhere else."

Anonymous

"Love what you have chosen to create or change it." Aviad Goz

The North in the N.E.W.S.® Compass is about creating your future. It is about a long-term strategic view. Navigating in the North is the essence of leadership. Leadership starts with providing direction and vision. This is true for self-leadership and team leadership, alike.

Being "Stuck" in the North means not knowing what is next, arriving at a dead end, not having any visibility of the future or the next step. This might happen for a lot of reasons: Completing a project, changing market situations, a life cycle coming to an end, or losing a job. Sometimes there is no visibility of the future because of an intense fear in the South about the future, which clouds our vision. Being "stuck" in the North can result from a lack of imagination, not being a "visionary" and having a Victim mentality with regard to the future.

The state of mind of the North is:
"I can create my own future by singularity of intention and vision"

People have different attitudes towards the future. They range from the reactive approach of being concerned about the future all the way to the very proactive attitude of being able to create the future.

- Being concerned about the future – At this level when people think about the future, they become concerned. Due to the complexity and instability of world affairs, people at this level become worried when they think about the future. They see themselves more as victims rather than people who can shape the future. This approach sometimes has deep cultural and historical roots. I can still remember my parents who survived the Holocaust and the great wars of the 20th century. Their approach to life was shaped in this way. They would always worry about what the future might bring, and who could blame them?

- Accepting the future as inevitable – This is a fatalistic approach based on the assumption that since we cannot influence the future, we must accept it. The belief is that we are all in the hands of greater forces i.e. destiny, the stars, God, karma and the like. Our will and choice do not matter much, as events will unfold by larger plans, fate or higher powers. Some cultures in the world educate their people with this approach, which allows easy control of the masses. As an example, I remember a time in India when I saw a crippled, amputated beggar sitting in the street. Out of compassion I put a coin in his hand. The senior Indian corporate HR manager who was with me that day was furious and told me "This is his Karma, his lesson in this life. Why do you want to intervene in that?"

I understood a deep cultural issue that says let circumstances rule your life, which brings to mind the famous saying: "Only dead fish flow with the stream".

- Readiness for the future – At this level, people do not believe that they can influence the future, but they believe that they can get ready for it. They can prepare a good retirement plan. They can store food. They can secure a good insurance policy. They can keep an evacuation kit in their car, etc. The main focus here is: "Be ready for whatever might happen". The Swiss culture is a very good example of this. Every house in Switzerland is equipped with a nuclear/ biological/ chemical underground shelter by law. When you ask Swiss people why they need such shelters as they have not had wars for 600 years, they answer "We need to be ready and probably because we are so ready, we do not have wars."
- Planning the future – At this level people adopt a more proactive approach and believe they can plan the future to some extent. They can plan next year's vacation. They can plan their career path. They can plan where they want to be in a few years' time. This is clearly demonstrated in the mainstream American culture.
- Creating the future – At this level, people believe they can create the future, first in their imagination and then by implementing their ideas practically and tangibly. This approach to life makes one a Creator rather than a Victim. People at this level assume very active roles in shaping the future.

As a good example, when Whoopi Goldberg won the Oscar, she gave a speech on the podium of the event in which she said "When I was a child, I saw myself standing here as I stand here today winning the Oscar. I came from a poor family, but I knew I would stand here one day." There were no chances for that to happen at that time, as black people and definitely black women did not win the Oscar back then.

Many people find this visionary approach somewhat challenging in this rapidly changing world. Yet the individuals who shape their reality and the reality of the world all come from the visionary approach.

If you think for a moment, everything around us in the human world was once in someone's mind. Everything from design to architecture, to the room you are sitting in, to the clothes you are wearing - all the way to the technology that you are using. All of it was created because someone at some point envisioned it all as viable in the future.

So, your departure point for the North journey is that you can create your future, your family's future and your organization's future.

You are the Creator – People who create their choice are often called visionaries and they shape our human world for better or for worse. They are the creative force of humankind.

Great people like Martin Luther King, Gandhi, Jules Verne, Leonardo Da Vinci, Steve Jobs, and Elon Musk, to name a few. Similarly, people who built empires and embarked on terrible wars were visionaries as well.

So, being a visionary does not guarantee the quality of visions or their morality. The morality or the reasons lie deep in the N.E.W.S.® East, the domain of why we choose what we do.

For you
Now, as we get ready for your journey in the North, let me share with you a real story of a personal journey in the North.

A personal journey in the North - The story of Michal
Michal was a bored speech therapist. She no longer liked her job and dreamed of doing something else with her life. We coached Michal with the N.E.W.S.® Coaching methodology. It became clear that her passions and core capabilities involved creating high quality healthy products. This "Inside – Out" drive had no expression in her professional life at the time.

Michal realized that she wanted to create healthy high-quality food for people. This was the direction she wanted to take. Her vision was to open a small organic dairy farm in a rural area and create the best possible line of goats' cheese. However, she lived with her family in a city and her reality was very far from dairy and farms. To help her we advised that she visit a dairy farm in Switzerland that also offers training in making delicious goats' cheese. We call this a "journey in time" to your desired future, to check how suitable it really is for you.

Michal went for a few weeks and came back very enthusiastic. "This is what I really want to do" she said, "I can see a high-quality dairy farm with a little restaurant next to it and people coming from all over specially to taste the cheese". Together, we built a practical model for how that could work. It was not going to be simple.

Michal quit her job and convinced her family to move with her to a small village. With her savings she bought a small house with a little shop attached to it and began to produce cheese from goats' milk that she acquired from neighboring farms. She kept learning constantly as she was and still is, a perfectionist.

Michal had to struggle with a lot of South to make her North come true. She had personal crises and difficulties all around. But she persisted. She started her own little herd of goats. She started trying different kinds of lines of cheeses.

Two years later Michal sent us a photo leaving her farm in a truck full of the first batch of cheese she produced for the market. The dream had come true.

But she didn't stop there. With great investment and persistent work, she kept developing, and soon people came from all over to buy her cheese and dine in the little restaurant.

Everything she did was of the best quality and with much passion. When we came over for a visit three years after she had started, Michal already felt that the place was too small for her.

Together with her we planned a move to a larger space for the cheese dairy farm and for the restaurant.

Our friends in a winery had exactly this kind of place available next to them. Michal moved and over a period of two years created the new place with a lot of vision and hard work.

She designed it and built most of it herself. The new place was beautiful and attractive. Since then, she has become famous throughout the country for her high-quality cheese, and she participates in international competitions. She has started winning medals and awards. The last we heard from Michal she had won 3 gold medals for her different types of cheese in the annual competition of the French association of cheese makers, the highest global award in the cheese industry. She later become a referee in this competition due to her unique experience and quality. Michal followed her heart and her dreams and with much hard work, struggle, and persistence, she created a new reality for the benefit of many.

www.shiratroim.co.il

YOUR PERSONAL JOURNEY IN THE NORTH

The personal journey in the North has three steps:
1. Discovering your "Direction of Greatness"
2. Creating your "Next Version"
3. Creating your "Practical Vision"

In order to embark on a meaningful impactful journey in the North, let me explain my unique approach to creating a personal future. When people think about the future there are many terms that they use, such as – vision, mission, direction, goals, objectives, strategy and more.

Very often these terms are confused or overlapping, and different people have many different views about their meanings.

I would like to propose clarity and a distinction between these terms. We work with them in the North as our practical tools in creating the North work.

For you
Imagine that a young person approaches you as an experienced adult. They tell you they have no idea what to do in the future. Their question to you is "Where should I start, if I want to shape my future?".

What would your answer be?

Some people might say "Start with what you like to do, or with what interests you". Others might say "Look for a profession that pays well and go and study it".

These two answers actually represent the two distinct approaches to the

North.

The first represents an "Inside – Out" approach focused on self-fulfillment and maximizing your contribution.

The second represents an "Outside – In" opportunistic approach that focuses on survival and financial reward and very often leads to mediocrity.

Your first step in the personal North - Setting a direction of Greatness.
While choosing a direction (a major decision we do not make very frequently), people generally use one of two models:

The "Survival Model" or the "Greatness Model".

A decision that arises from the Survival Model is the result of answers to some externally driven questions, which people then try to conform to, from within:

Where is the money? Where can I get a better car?

Or where can I get better conditions from my employer?

What will it take for me to access money, car, or conditions etc.?

What can I do to get this money or conditions, regardless of whether I like doing it or if I am even good at it?

In poor economies, many decisions are based on the demands of necessity for survival - Where is the food? Where can I find water? How can I feed my family?

These survival questions will lead to survival choices. If you were born in Sub Saharan Africa and the only place to work to provide food for your family was in a local diamond mine, you would surely work in that mine. You would work in whatever role you could find, just to survive.

In some situations, and economic realities, it is the only realistic model to follow. For centuries, the majority of humanity had to follow this model to survive.

In the more developed economies, there is much more choice. In such economies, the survival model is an anachronistic default approach, which does not allow real choice.

It always leads to mediocrity over time.

People who do whatever it takes to earn a living, end up with very low motivation and little or no engagement in the workplace. People who do what they are not really good at, end up adding very little value to their workplace or business. Their survival approach keeps them very small and very dependent in their roles. They wait for the working day to be over, or for the week to end, or for the working year to be over.

They count the minutes, hours and days, so that they can finally go home and "live their lives".

"Survival/Mediocrity Model"

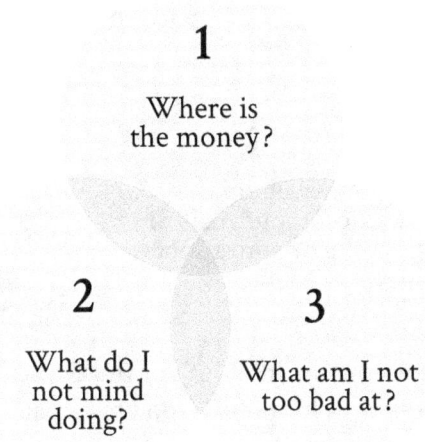

This approach is still very common in the world today. Studies indicate that 70%- 80% of the world's population still use it, consciously or unconsciously, as their main approach to choosing their path in life. This is often encouraged by parents and family, the approach they grew up with in a world that was much less developed economically, a world that offered fewer choices than our world today.

For you
Can you recognize elements of such approach in the way you chose your direction in life or career?

A much more effective approach for your direction in life, would be to first define the right direction for you based on who you really are as an individual. When such a direction is set after much enquiry and self-searching, preferably with a coach, we call it an "Inside – Out" approach. This approach is formulated as the "Greatness Model."

The "Greatness Model"

1
What am I passionate about?

2
What am I born to do?

3
What are the needs and goals of the organization?

(Adapted from Jim Collins)

Setting a direction from the "Inside-Out", or the Greatness model, was first introduced by Jim Collins in his book "Good to Great".

Originally this model described how successful companies moved from being average to becoming great in their performance, to arrive at leadership positions in their markets.

In his groundbreaking study Jim Collins detailed the questions the leaders of these organizations asked themselves. Their first in-bound question was:

"What are we passionate about?"

and the second in-bound question that they asked themselves was: "What were we born to do?"

The meeting point between these two creates the "Direction of Greatness", their True North.

This is the "Big Arrow" that would allow those companies to navigate to their full potential and leverage their unique drive and talent in the marketplace. This model when applied to companies creates a powerful drive and a tremendous ability to focus on the uniqueness of the particular company.

In a similar way this model is applicable to individuals. When an individual addresses these questions, with or without the assistance of a coach, they embark on a journey of self- discovery. This journey will lead them to realize their unique potential and greatness and plan their direction accordingly. The meeting point between authentic, long-term passions on the one hand, and the core competences on the other hand, leads to the discovery of a "Direction of Greatness" for the person.

It is important to note that neither passion nor core capabilities alone will suffice. It is the intersection between these two that will indicate a direction of greatness.

In the model of greatness, passions are everything that the person loves to do, is inspired by, and is deeply interested in. What they are passionate about, not for gain or glory, but just because of who they are. Deep passions can be recognized at a young age and need to be separated from education or heritage. Parents can observe in their young children the emerging love of nature or the passion to dance or the attraction to physical challenges or the deep interest in solving complex problems.

It is almost the mission of parents to observe those passions in a child and nurture them, whether the parents like them or not. In addition to passions we look for talents and core capabilities other than those a person develops on their journey. We look for those talents and capabilities that are innate. Those that were always present. These core capabilities can later be enhanced and developed. We look for everything the person is gifted with. Everything they do at the level of excellence and with relative ease.

These core capabilities can be anything from hosting people, to arranging a space, to entrepreneurial approach, to therapy skills.

These two core elements - passions and core capabilities, are there from birth. They are much like your unique DNA. Every person has a unique combination of passions and core capabilities or talents from birth. It is up to parents, mentors or coaches to help discover them. Every person has their potential Greatness, even if they do not see it as such.

For you
Explore your passions and core talents.

Write them down. Look for the most essential ones.

Where do they intersect?
What does that say about your natural greatness?
Can you do the same process for your children?

Once discovered, the journey is about becoming more and more accurate in realizing this meeting point, this "sweet spot" - your direction of greatness.

This direction of greatness can be expressed in a "direction sentence". This sentence is combined from the core words of your passions and capabilities. This sentence is like a mission statement that describes the overall direction of how you can express your own greatness.

Over time you need to learn how to express this direction of greatness and even how to best leverage it, for this is the very best of us. The best that we can contribute to others and the world.

This is also our best option of fulfilling ourselves in this life in most cases it is also our best shot at economic success.

Our direction of Greatness also represents the best of us for the people that we work with and for the organizations that we work for. When others witness a person who is passionate and capable, it is inspiring for them. For who can love anyone who is bitter with what they do?"

Let me share a useful analogy.

Take an object– let's say a teacup, specially designed to contain and carry hot liquids, with that little handle on the side so you don't burn your fingers. The weight, structure, materials all serve this purpose of making it easy and comfortable to drink hot beverages.

Now, this teacup could certainly also be used for other purposes – a doorstop, paper weight, even a weapon to throw at someone.

The cup can be used for all these purposes. But none of them are the ultimate original use for which the teacup was created and designed.

Likewise, with a person, they can use themselves and their system for an endless number of purposes. They can be enlisted as a soldier. They can become a waiter in a restaurant to make money. They can work in construction.

Their government or society can use them for all kind of purposes.

However, the person might have not been actually created and designed for most of these purposes.

So, can you take a person who is naturally a great art designer and make them into a clerk at the bank? You can do that, and the person might even be ok at their job. But this is not the best use of their talents and passions.

It is a waste. It will cause lack of fulfillment, little or no contribution and a frustrated life journey.

This is much like the teacup that can be used for so many other purposes and yet its optimal usage is singular.

I know so many people in this situation where their choices and behavior are very far away from who they are intrinsically and who they could have become. They earn their living, but they are mostly miserable. I have a friend who is a gifted sculptor. He could not find the practical model to live from this talent. So, instead he organizes and stages weddings. Every conversation I have with this person always centers around the deep frustration and longing to create, sculpt and build large structures of beauty.

Here are some examples for "Direction sentences" that some people created. "To build sustainable business through people development".

"To lead individuals and organizations to breakthroughs". "To create environments of growth with people".

"To create friendly interfaces between people and new technologies". "To manufacture high quality and healthy foods for people".

For you
What will yours be?

In the North, we always start with setting a direction. We attempt to find an "Inside – Out" direction that is unique to the person or to the team. We can call it "The True North". Many argue that future planning should start with a vision. From my experience with thousands of individuals, teams and companies, I find this approach to be misleading in most cases. Most people or organizations when trying to start a North process towards the future, set a vision that may have nothing to do with them and who they really are. It is usually copied or generic, influenced by fashion, trends, advertisement, ambition and competition. It is often just as generic as: "to lead our industry", "to be the first-choice provider" etc.

People see themselves sitting in the future on the CEO chair, whether it suits who they truly are or not.

Companies see themselves entering and capturing new markets with new services or products whether it is suitable for them or not. We call this approach, the "Outside – In" approach.

It usually leads to futile efforts and disappointment after spending a lot of time and resources.

Even when it is "successful" this approach requires a lot of drive and effort. It drains the people that take part in the endeavor and certainly does not leverage their true talents and passions. Everyone aspires to succeed.

I propose here that the best success is the one that brings to full potential who and what you truly are.

This kind of "Direction of Greatness" which we also call "Your True North" will give you a luminous path to follow. It provides clear boundaries that help you discern opportunities that come your way, by asking:

"Is this an opportunity for me?"

It gives a clear prism of choice, if an opportunity that came your way is "in or out" of your authentic direction. Therefore, it becomes a powerful decision- making prism and tool. It is like a guide for those in the land of the blind to see.

The other option, of course, is to turn your passions and core capabilities into a hobby. It could be gardening, yachting, playing music, etc. There is nothing wrong with that and many people do just that. The only problem with this approach is that it limits a person's focus and contribution to a hobby and limits their impact to satisfy mainly themselves or their family. Imagine if Mozart had turned his musical genius into a hobby of playing once a week in a local bar in Vienna. Or if Steve Jobs had turned his passion and talent for technological aesthetics into a hobby of attending calligraphy class once a week.

We would have missed some sublime music and the amazing, beautiful technologies we have today.

These people and others heeded their passions. They leveraged their talents. They diligently pursued the expression of their constant drive from "inside – out" and created for us, some of the best of what the world has to offer.

The many thousands of people and companies I have worked with over the past few decades, express how dramatic and significant the discovery of their direction of greatness has been for them. This discovery eventually leads to a high level of self-fulfillment and outstanding successes.

It leads to optimum results through enhanced contribution.

This process creates highly motivated and fulfilled people. They usually score very high on the subjective well-being index. Research also shows that people who follow this path are even less likely to suffer the risk factors for heart disease. It is also a most rewarding experience for colleagues to work with such a person and for the organization that employs them.

For you
To finalize this first step, think about yourself.

To what extent do you actually express your Greatness in the work you do today or in the way you do it?

To what degree do you bring your natural greatness to work?

If the first step in the Personal North gave you some insights, the second step is even more practical.

In this step you will come from your Greatness to meet the changing reality.

YOUR SECOND STEP IN THE PERSONAL JOURNEY IN THE NORTH

Personal strategy and practical models to meet the changing reality.

Most people fail when trying to translate their Greatness into a viable practical model that will allow them to work and thrive by doing what they love and are good at.

In this step I will help you create that elusive meeting point between what you are passionate about doing and what the world is passionate about getting.

I mentioned that the word Strategy comes from the Greek word Strategos - the leader of an army who in ancient times led the battle by standing elevated above the plain (strata) of the battlefield to view it in order to make informed decisions about moving his forces from this broader perspective. Hence, strategy is the ability to reach major decisions from a higher point of view. Strategy, in this case has to do with finding the practical meeting point between the Constant and the Variable. This requires a thorough view of self and of the environment. The meeting point moves as the variable moves. The strategic approach will be to explore practical models or strategic drivers for the next phase or even the next version of yourself to be released into the changing reality.

"Your next version" is a very contemporary way of thinking about your Personal North in a fast-changing reality. I first used this term in 2012 and it has become a trend ever since.

This represents a very practical and strategic approach to constant and changing elements in the development of the North for individuals, teams and organizations alike.

The Constant
The process of transformation towards manifesting your "Direction of

Greatness" can be erratic or disruptive.

To create the next version of yourself frequently can take you to totally unaligned and non-productive places.

Your journey of fulfillment and success should follow a constant line. Moving away from this line will cause a crazy zigzag effect that will lead nowhere.

One of the people I have coached had that syndrome. Every year or two, Gordon would get bored with what he was doing. He liked the excitement of new things and could not sustain anything for very long. For two years he was into alternative medicine and practiced various approaches. Then he became excited about music and trained as a D.J. Once this started working, he got bored and moved to cooking organic food. He opened a small restaurant only to discover that managing the staff and handling purchasing was boring and tedious. He closed the restaurant and then became interested in drones and photography and the story goes on…

So, interestingly enough, even in a constantly changing world, you should pursue a consistent, constant line.

The "constant" should include your overall purpose for being, your "True" North direction and core values.

This "constant" will allow you paradoxically to be agile and flexible with the changing world around you without getting dispersed. This is much like a strong backbone that allows flexibility and agility for the entire body. Self-transformation or growth can be disruptive if there is no constant line in it.

"The direction of Greatness" in line with a person's uniqueness does not really change over time.

If anything, it gets clearer and more accurate as you investigate it and experiment with it over time.

This constant direction of greatness gives you a domain in which there are many options on the one hand and very clear boundaries on the other.

Inside this domain you can experiment, try many options and transform as needed.

Outside of this domain you get lost, following transient fashions and changing winds of hot topics adored by the ignorance of the crowd.

It is therefore imperative to discover this constant direction of Greatness which allows for coherent choice over time.

For you
When you set a direction that is aimed at reaching your full potential, then and only then can we discuss the vision of success. Vision in this case answers the question "What will success look like in the future if I follow the direction of my true potential and Greatness?" This approach can create what could become your "True North".

The Variable

The constant direction of Greatness meets the changing world. To do so, there must be a variable element. To stick only to the constant will result in rigidity. To stick only to the variable will result in excessive flexibility and dispersion. Hence the meeting point of the constant and the variable is crucial. The variables that change are numerous. Here are a few elements that change constantly and need to be taken into consideration regularly.

Life Cycles

As people pass through the years, they undergo cycles of change that can be described as "seasons of life". I found that different people have different cycles. Some go through a major change every 12 years, others every 7 or even 3 years. It is as if some large clock is ticking somewhere and cycles are completed.

Then a major change is needed. Beyond that, at different points in life people have varying levels of energy, openness to learn, established experience, appetite for risk, need for safety, acceptance of oneself and so on.

Ancient cultures called this phenomenon the "7 ages of man", or "four stages of life" for the Hindu, and similar ones.

If we are the main tool of making our journey, it is important to evolve over time. As an example, a young dynamic man in his 20's can conquer new spaces and climb mountains. The same person 40 years later can become a good coach or mentor for young mountain climbers and 20 years later gather his memories in a book to inspire other mountain climbers.

For you
Can you work out your natural cycle of change? Where are you in that cycle now?

Needs

Your needs change, not just with age but also because of life circumstances, including the needs of your family.

Your young children grow up and leave home. Grandchildren are born and often live in distant cities.

Your spouse relocates to another country, your mother becomes ill and has to have dedicated care. You yourself might go through various external and internal changes. Here are few examples of changes:

You get bored at your job. You have a need to be more mobile or on the contrary, you need to settle down after a long period of movement. A new subject interests you. You need a higher income for the mortgage you have just taken. You want to spend the winter in a warmer climate, and so on.

So many needs change as life unfolds that require us to adapt.

For you
How would you describe your current needs?
Does your current practical model allow you to meet these needs satisfactorily?

External Changes
As indicated before, we live in times of accelerated change.

Each change requires adaptation, fine tuning or modification. Let me share my own story. When I was a child, we didn't have a landline phone at home. We had to wait on a standby list for 7 years to get one. International calls were ridiculously expensive. Years passed till the first heavy Motorola cell phones appeared. I had one. It was like a big stick. It was very unfriendly but heralded a dramatic revolution in how people communicated. Lighter cell phones appeared, smartphones, emails, Skype, Zoom, WhatsApp, free IP calls with video, new generations of smartphones appeared with numerous applications. We have all become attached to smartphones as an extension of our hands. Most people are totally addicted and cannot envision life without this device. When it is taken from them, they experience withdrawal symptoms. In my life, I went through a revolution in communication, like you perhaps, and had to adjust to fast response, real time work, extensive accessibility and more.

Another example: My first job was in a pharma company. One day a huge machine appeared that was assembled in what was named "the computer room." The computer was the size of the entire room. Four people handled the massive computer with white gloves and face masks, as if they were working in the Center for Infectious Diseases. It used to issue sales reports once a week. Nowadays in my home I have a smart computer with a giant screen, and my laptop, my ipad and my smartphone are all connected and synchronized. The funny thing is that the old computer that needed a huge room didn't have even 1% of the computing power my smartphone has now.

I grew up in a small town of refugees and holocaust survivors. As I developed at work, I was exposed to the whole country's population which was varied culturally. As I moved on, I started to work in other countries, slowly learning their different cultures, paradigms and habits. In the last decade, I have owned a company that operates in more than 40 countries, each different from a cultural standpoint, from a human standpoint, with different religions, customs and lifestyles. I had to expand my bandwidth to contain all that, to adapt to all of it.

I think these three illustrations of communication, technology and globalization, are examples of the era in which we live. Take as an example a real estate agent who works in the old traditional ways without any social media activity. They are simply not relevant anymore. Maybe the best illustration would be the "Bellboys" working in elevators in the 50's and 60's. They have now been extinct for more than 60 years. The changes do not occur at the same time in all geographic locations. Some parts of the world are now moving from the agricultural age to the industrial age where millions move to cities to work in factories and plants. In other parts of the world there is a movement from the industrial age to the knowledge age where people move to smarter global companies. In other parts the knowledge age and technological companies rule and move on to AI domains, where most workers will not be needed, unless they are savvy, creative and innovative. All these movements leave behind millions of people who cannot adapt and feel that they were thrown "out of the line of opportunity". This creates social unrest that gives rise to phenomena like Brexit, or the election of Donald Trump and other leaders that promise to fix the problem, but of course, fail to deliver.

Although different parts of the world go through different processes, global connectivity insures that globally information will be shared rapidly, and broadly. In the face of all this you need to make your choices wisely.

For you

Which external changes do you need to take into account as you move to your next step in your life?

For you to be able to put all of that into a practical model let me introduce in depth the concept of "Your next version"

YOUR NEXT VERSION

What is common to all these roles?

School teacher, professional gardener, professional dancer, choreographer, army commander, entertainment group, combat doctor, doctor in hospitals, medical rep, army psychologist, consultant, waiter, restaurant manager, biologist, researcher, personal development guide, head of personal development school, team leader, product manager, marketing manager, owner of 2 startup companies, owner of a tourist resort, partner in a tourist agency, university lecturer, keynote speaker, trainer of Fortune 100 companies, coach for CEO'S, facilitator for leadership teams, CEO of a global company, chairman of two companies, partner in a winery, partner in a bar, real estate investor, author of books, creator of models, builder, board member, leadership consultant, and a CVO of a global company.

What is common to all the roles on this list is ME!

I have held all these different roles in my career of 40+ years and I plan to fulfill more roles in the years to come.

I do not feel tired or exhausted, not at all, on the contrary, I feel fulfilled. I feel that I have released many versions of myself into the changing reality. I feel that I have lived thoroughly, and I have probably expressed different potentials that were in me, some obvious and some hidden. And I know many others who have changed their roles and even occupations a few times in their lifetimes.

What is your list of different roles you have fulfilled over the years? Do they present the different facets of your potential?

What an amazing era we live in where people can evolve into so many roles in a single lifetime!

Just 50 years ago, the majority of humanity followed in their parents' footsteps. The son of the farmer became a farmer, the child of the blacksmith pursued that tradition. If you came from a warrior's dynasty, there was a good chance you would become a warrior.

So, what has changed that allows and even demands that people change jobs, career paths and even direction a few times in one lifetime?

Some reasons are obvious.

Life Expectancy – We simply live much longer. In the beginning of the 20th century people had only one shot at a career for 20-25 years and then they retired. The average lifespan was only 45. We now live to be over 80 years old. Most of the young readers will live to be 90 years old and more. People continue to work and create until a much more advanced age. In 60 long years of working and creating, a person can do much more than in the short 20-25 years that our grandparents had.

Mobility – Our mobility is without precedence. 40-50 years ago, the vast majority of humanity lived all their lives in the village or neighborhood where they were born. Nowadays when I ask participants in workshops "who lives in the village or neighborhood where they were born?" often very few hands are raised and sometimes not even one. We move, we relocate, our spouses relocate, we move to other cities, other countries and that dramatically affects the career paths that we develop. In the world today we have now a new group of young people – Digital Nomads. These are people who travel and work from a distance. Currently their numbers are estimated around 200 million. It is estimated that this number will double in the next few years.

Choice – spoken of before, the amount of choice we have is totally unprecedented and as Peter Ducker put it "we are totally not prepared for it".

In the developed world at least, we can study anything we choose. We can choose any career path; we can change jobs as many times as we want. We are faced with endless coices, and it can be confusing.

In the US by the age of 32, young people on an average, have already changed jobs six times. We are not limited in choice and that is both a blessing and a curse.

For you
How do you choose when the choice is infinite?

How do you act from abundance and not from scarcity?

Change – It is predicted that half of today's jobs will not exist in 10 years' time. Young people study and prepare themselves for jobs that will no longer exist, such as drivers, insurance agents, travel agents, teachers of different kinds, and more. Robots are coming into the workspace. How do you navigate yourself or your business, so you do not become obsolete?

I see so many people at the age of 45-50 (midlife) who have become obsolete and been made redundant. They cannot find their way back to the workforce or into being useful and that is very sad indeed. This drama impacts entire families and often communities. This is happening more and more globally.

A recent study conducted by the OECD shows that most teenagers still dream of working in jobs that are going to be extinct in a decade. These are the same jobs their parents envisaged. This is a short-sighted approach that will lead those teenagers to a dead end.

Evolution – Humanity is changing rapidly. For many hundreds of years in the middle ages, humanity did not change much. Today people leap forward in one lifetime more than our ancestors could over generations. The levels of intelligence, innovation, and consciousness that can be connected to and translated are unprecedented.

I know a person born to a poor family in the Andes mountains in South America who at the age of 40 became a world-famous lecturer on the global stage. I know another person who was born in a poor neighborhood in Calcutta, India, to a family that sold shoes in a small booth in the local market. This person at the age of 50 was the Dean of Harvard Business School, an author of global best-selling business books and a coach of global leading CEOs. Once upon a time such stories were fairy tales. Nowadays it is a common reality that occurs more and more. Evolution has to do with adapting to changing circumstances. Under this definition we are in a time of evolution. Take a look at small children being born and growing up now. They are digitally savvy, fast, clever. It comes with negative side effects but clearly these children are different from children that were born 50 years ago.

How best to make choices in times of change?

For you

What do you need to change for the next stage of your journey to fulfillment and

contribution?
What level of change is needed?

This question might require some thinking and research and is not simple. The answers might lead you to four different levels of change and update.
1. Minor change – minor change and adaptation. This kind of change might include learning a new skill, acquiring new knowledge, specializing in a topic, small changes in location, activity, expression, market etc. A real story- Leonie was a writer and a translator for children's books in English. At some point she realized that the market was shrinking. She decided to expand her services and translate business and management books for mainstream readers. She took a course in Business English to learn the required current vocabulary. These services of Leonie's became a success.

2. Major change - Sometimes a minor change is not enough. The meeting point of your constant line with the variable changing environment requires a major change. A major change might mean relocation, serious professional change, acquiring new expertise, moving to another market, a change in the way you do things. Major change is not easy. Usually the younger you are, the easier it is. Sometimes people mature and some of them move into survival mode and a "keep it going" type of drive. In that mode it becomes more difficult to change. Yet sometimes it is really necessary due to internal and external circumstances. A real story - David was a third-generation pharmacist. He inherited a small family pharmacy in a small town. He studied pharmacology and started to run the family business. The first few years were pretty good. There was a solid loyal clientele. Every month he earned well. He decided on a minor change and renovated the old pharmacy, brought in new products and hired an employee specialized in natural products. It went well, and David loved his job and his little pharmacy. A few good years passed, and a national chain of drugstores opened a branch less than 500 meters from David's pharmacy. Business immediately declined. The new branch was huge. It had a large variety of products. It had lower prices and an aggressive marketing campaign. Even David's "loyal" customers came by more rarely. David looked at the trends and realized that it was a national phenomenon, not likely to change. The large chains were

running the small pharmacies out of business. When he reached the point of not being able to draw a decent monthly salary, David had to make a choice. He could become an employee as a pharmacist. He could join the national chain and work for them, but he chose another option. The trend of natural medicine, supplements and organic food was growing in his town. He decided to keep his pharmacy running, but to make it highly specialized. He went on to create a "healthy pharmacy" specializing in natural medicines, aromatherapy, organic foods and homeopathy. He took some advanced courses, hired the right staff of ND's and created a new type of pharmacy. He kept his passion to help people. This was a new practical model in his line of greatness. The "healthy pharmacy" concept was very successful. So much so, that a few years later David opened another "healthy pharmacy" in a nearby town and now he is on the way opening his third branch in a large city not far away.

3. No change at all – you might be in the middle of a chapter in your life that requires no change. You need to move on and complete that chapter before looking for further change.

A real story - Nancy was a software engineer in a large IT company. She was promoted to project manager. It took her a few months to put together a team, learn and plan the project and set out to achieve it. This was a very intensive process. She had to learn a lot, both professionally and as a young first-time manager. Some months later Nancy got an offer from the company to move on to lead a larger project that was about to start.

Nancy declined the offer. She felt that she had just got the current project up and running. She was still learning a lot every day. She felt deeply that to make another change to a new larger project was premature for her. She was aware of the fact that she was still a manager in training.

For you.
Take a look at your last phase in life since the last change you made. What name would you give to this period? Think about your situation. What kind of a change is needed now? A major change? A minor change? Or no change at all?

4. Create your own next version. Sometimes the internal changes and the changes in the environment require more than a major change. The meeting point between your constant direction and the changing reality is no longer relevant. When that happens, a larger choice is at stake. Will you dare to recreate a whole new version of yourself or will you become irrelevant and extinct like the dinosaurs?

A next version type of change will require a change of profession, change of career path, major change of mindset, skillset and toolset. The most important aspect in creating your own next version is to remain aligned to your constant direction of greatness. Within that direction look for new practical solutions. Careful not to replace your direction of Greatness with survival and mediocrity model solutions.

A real story - George was a software engineer; he loved technology. He loved to learn, and he also loved to teach. He was very good at innovating, computing and instructing. He started his career as a trainer in a high-tech college. He gave courses in various computing languages. At some point he got an offer he could not refuse – to join a high-tech company specializing in SAS - Software As Service for the telecom industry. George worked for that company for 15 years. He became a team leader. Then a project manager. He ran global projects and spent much time away from home. The projects would take him to India or to Ireland for two weeks at a time, and then after a short break, to the Ukraine for six weeks and so on. Meanwhile George's family grew. He had three children. However, due to his international projects, he only got to see them one weekend a month. Even then, it was only for a short time before they went to sleep. The pressure at work was intense. There were daily crises to be solved. There were many customers to visit. George was now over 40 years old. He had an excellent salary, some savings, but he was worn out and tired and above all, missed his family. At one point the company had a town hall meeting for all project leaders. There were 400 of them in the hall. The CEO emphasized the competition in the market and the need to lower costs. All project leaders were asked to reduce their head counts by 20% and look for younger cheaper workers to replace some of their senior mature "more expensive" programmers. This was a very difficult moment for George.

He had to let go of fifteen of his best people. This was very tough for George emotionally. These were people he had been working with for many years. Some had actually become his friends.

He had to recruit five new programmers fresh from college, train them all over again and keep the same level of production and delivery as before. This was an excruciating experience that lasted a few months. Then George heard that the company was beginning to lay off senior project leaders and replace them with new younger and "cheaper" project leaders. George connected the dots. He realized that to look for a new job as a tech project leader at the age of 45 was almost too late.

He had to do something and do it soon. He took a three-week break from work, spent time with his family and thought a great deal. After the long break, George resigned from the company and left with his stock options.

The next thing he did surprised everyone who did not know him very well. He took some of his savings, hired a skilled kindergarten teacher and opened his own kindergarten next to his home.

It was a special kindergarten with emphasis on technological education for children. George was now the owner of a "techy" kindergarten. In his new business he earned much less, but he felt that he won back his life and his family. George combined his love of teaching with his technological skills and created a totally new version of himself. The kindergarten became a success and the waiting list is two years long. Actually, some parents pre-register their children at birth.

George now works five hours a day. He has a lot of fun and great activities with the kids and even with their parents. He spends the afternoons and evenings with his family. They play together and create small technological projects and solve math problems. He has long vacations. The fatigue and burnout have disappeared completely. He even started to take two evening courses every week. One course for advanced cyber technologies and one about new paths in childhood education, keeping alive his passion for learning and education.

For you
Could you envisage such a change if you were in George's place?

What does it take to create a whole new version of yourself in the North?
1. Reading the map.
2. Boldly facing the inevitable.
3. The ability to create and carve the new version.
4. Remaining loyal to your constant direction of greatness.
5. Having the courage to make the "leap".
6. Being hopeful and optimistic.
7. Good planning and good execution.
8. The right timing.

Creating your own next version is not a trivial choice. Sometimes it is like jumping from a cruise ship into the ocean hoping you will find a little boat there.

And sometimes it is simply inevitable.

A point of awareness: the variable circumstances can be very confusing. There is a huge amount of data to be processed to understand trends and where things are heading. Try to focus on the few key elements that will impact your life, your journey and your choices. Sift out all the noise, the social media, the too much information and the fake news. Try to find some wise people and consult with them. And finally, never assume that you really understand the full picture of reality. At best you have an educated guess. That will be good enough to lead you forward.

For you
Are you approaching the point where this order of change might be needed? Do you have the courage and the support needed for such a change?

If so, do not delay. Markets and social trends are less forgiving than ever before.

Welcome now into the third step in the North. Whether no change is needed, or your life journey requires a full creation of your next version, step three is still vital for you.

STEP THREE IN THE PERSONAL JOURNEY IN THE NORTH - PRACTICAL VISION

The final step in the North is to create a practical vision. There are many different views about what a vision is. Some would say it is a kind of mission. Some will say it is an inspiring sentence of future possibilities. For me, a vision is as simple as it sounds - a picture of the future. The main question here is: If you put next practical model to work, what will your reality look like three or five years from now?

It is a picture of a best-case scenario in the future. It needs to be specific, tangible and attainable. It needs to be written in a positive way and be the right magnitude for you to try and achieve it.

All of these are required because of the way the human brain functions. Our brain processes data from the senses and creates for us a replica - a "picture of reality" in our mind. That picture provides us the intelligence of how to proceed in life.

Having a practical vision repeatedly creates for the mind a unique situation. When we begin to have in our mind a repetitive picture of a future reality, which is already tangible, practical, and attainable, our mind now has two pictures of reality. The current one and the future one. This situation is highly uncomfortable for the mind.

The mind actually tries to close the gap between the two pictures of reality by enlisting the brain's capacity and capabilities.

This means that your brain has more and more ideas on how to close the gap. You are more sensitized to new opportunities in this domain and your brain actively searches for solutions. Therefore, the process of getting to that future reality is accelerated.

You will find many stories about prisoners of war that survive the horrors of being captive, by repeatedly exercising imagining the future reality they yearned for. This allowed them to overcome their current reality and survive.

A practical vision is based on imagination. Most children have imagination and as they grow up, often the education systems destroy their imagination by over-emphasizing a realistic, mathematical and practical approach. The child who daydreams in class and imagines himself roaming free in nature outside the classroom, will probably not get much positive feedback from teachers.

I am often surprised how very few people have a picture of themselves in the future. What do they want to be? What do they want to do? What do they want to have? I wonder how they navigate through life if they do not know where they want to go.

For you
Do you have a picture of the future in your mind? What do you envision?
How did you create that particular picture?

Here is something I really believe in:

"If a person does not create their own future, others will do it for them". It might be governments, social movements, leaders, political parties, parents, spouses or bosses. Someone will enter that vacuum and create a future reality for them.

For you
Wouldn't it be better to be in the "driver's seat" of creating your own future?

The future is created in the North, first by imagination and then with planning and execution in the West.

When I realized that most people do not have a picture of future reality in their minds, I was propelled to research the reasons for that. Here is what I found to be the main reasons:

Fear – when a person dares to have a bold vision for the future, there is a chance they will fail. Most people are afraid of failure, so they don't dare.

"The greater danger for most of us lies not in setting our aim too high and falling short, but in setting our aim too low and achieving our mark." Michelangelo wisely wrote.

Availability – people are buried alive in their daily mundane stressful life. Most do not have the availability of mind to rise above the pressing daily requirements to project any far-reaching future reality.

Knowledge – I believe that many people are simply not aware of the power of imagination. Deliberate guided imagination of a future reality is not a creative tool that most people use regularly. Very often this is due to lack of education or awareness.

Yet people use their imagination when they plan a vacation.

They imagine what it will be like. They use their imagination when they design their home and try to imagine how it will look.

However, they do not apply the same tool of imagination to create their most important project – their own life.

To help people who do not have much imagination, we use a trick. We use "Left brain" tools to stimulate imagination in the "Right brain".

We might ask them to write an annual report to summarize a good year three years in the future.

We might ask them to plan an ideal week three years from now in their Outlook system.

When people are engaged using tools such as a report or a weekly Outlook system, most can allow themselves to imagine.

People come up with great results from this kind of exercise.

They manage to create in their minds a desirable future reality in line with their Greatness.

For you
What will your yearly report be for concluding a successful year, three years from now? What will you be doing then? What will you achieve? What will you have? What will your financial situation be? What will your relationships be like? And so on...

As this book is designed to accompany your journey, at the end of each chapter, I will offer a deeper view for those who might be interested.

ONE STEP DEEPER INTO THE PERSONAL NORTH

Many argue that a journey to the future must start with a vision. In my research I tried to find the source of people's visions. It became clear that most people adopt visions from the media, from other peoples' experience, from what is trendy or from what their peers are doing.

A copycat vision is dangerous and will not serve you well. The reason is that someone else's vision might not be suitable for you.

You might invest years in trying to achieve it, just to discover that it is empty and has nothing to do with you. This is when I came up with the idea of the "Inside – Out" approach instead of the "Outside – In" approach.

This is why I start the North personal journey with "Passions" and "Born to Do's". These two are your intrinsic markers. They are "Who you really are".

From those two authentic elements you create a direction of Greatness. From that you create your next version and the next practical model. If you follow this direction from the Inside – Out, if you put your next practical model to work, what will success look like – three years, five years, or even ten years down the road?

So, for us at N.E.W.S.®, practical vision comes last.

We also urge people not to delay making their visions real, but to start as soon as they can. Often that will involve overcoming a deeply entrenched South.

The realization of a powerful vision of future reality can start here and now. It often does not take a long time to materialize. You have enormous capability to create in the field of all possibilities. It is then that you need to follow through in your West.

As Walt Disney profoundly said, "If you can dream it, you can create it".

I meet people years after going through this self-navigation process and they are often excited to tell me "Do you remember that practical vision that I wrote down seven years ago? Well, you will not believe this, but it came true and I even went beyond what I then thought was possible".

For you
Now it is your turn....

THE N.E.W.S.® PERSONAL JOURNEY IN THE EAST - INTRODUCTION

East sayings

"From the East comes the light" a Latin saying

"If the wind in your sails is strong enough, you can sail to any distance" Aviad Goz

"He who has a strong enough "Why?" can bear almost any "How?" Fredrich Nietzsche

The East deals with meaning, values, motivation and drivers.

"Why do we want to go in this direction?"

For you
Welcome into the N.E.W.S.® journey in the East. It is fundamentally different from the Journey in the North. The North journey is strategic and creative. The East journey is deep and profound, energizing and stimulating.

The N.E.W.S.® East personal journey is fundamentally about energy. It is about motivation, engagement and drive. It is about the engine that provides individuals the power to travel the distance to their desired North. Without such an engine, the North is but a good intention seldom achieved. There are two types of motivation.
1. Extrinsic –from the outside. This includes salary, bonuses, stock options, recognition, promotion and others. This type of motivation is dependent on external sources.
2. Intrinsic –from within. This includes belief, purpose, meaning, values.

This type of motivation is independent of external sources. It comes from within. It is powerful and far reaching.

The N.E.W.S.® East deals with intrinsic motivations that can take you all the way to achieve your North. Every management theory recommends a mix of extrinsic and intrinsic motivation factors to motivate and engage employees. Often the intrinsic motivations are forgotten or are not part of what drives a person. In that case the person becomes disconnected from who and what they are, and are driven only by external forces.

Over time this might lead to fatigue, burnout, loss of meaning, and depression.

The East deals with the question "Why?" Why are you going in that direction?" "Why do you do what you do?" "Why this and not something else?".

It was Socrates who discovered the power of the question "Why?". This question searches for the deeper meaning. It looks for the root cause. It is different from "What?" or "How?" or "Where?" Socrates used to ask the people in his town the question "Why?" five consecutive times about what they think or do. That would lead him to expose people's deeper reasons and drivers. Apparently, people in his town did not like it a great deal because eventually he was poisoned.

So, the question "Why?", is designed to locate the core drivers, motivations and engagement of individuals in working out what will drive their direction, strategy and vision.

The East is the energy and the light (yellow like the sun rising from the East) that drives processes.

"From the East comes the light; from the West comes the law" Latin maxim.

The East represents the deepest origins of authentic motivations. Intrinsic motivation comes from a deep inner connection to one's values, purpose and reason for existence. It is concerned with those elements that a person values most, such as deep beliefs or their inner calling. The work in the East on the personal level is to reconnect people to their inner motivation and a personal sense of meaning. The East is the engine that develops long- term meaningful drivers towards fulfillment and realization.

A good example for the East is a person who serves as a volunteer in a non-profit organization such as an environmental movement. That person resonates with the cause and mission of the movement. He or she does not usually do it for money or recognition or promotion. And yet they might invest the best of their time and efforts for that cause because they believe deeply in the need to save the planet from the unfortunate effects of the human industrial and technological eras.

THE PERSONAL JOURNEY IN THE EAST

The story of Frederic.
Frederic was a high-ranking French executive, the CEO of a large insurance company. I met Frederic in one of our workshops. Frederic asked to be coached. When I asked him why he needed to be coached, he answered that he lacked well- being. In our meetings I tried to understand Frederic's actual situation. Frederic was at that time a wealthy man. He was married. He had a house and a castle not far from Paris. He had his own yacht in the Côte d'Azur and a little winery in Burgundy. All of these were his hobbies outside his job. He had 40 days' vacation every year and spent them by the sea or in his vineyards. "How come you lack well-being with all that?" I asked in sincere surprise.

"All of this does not give me well-being" he answered. "I feel detached, empty, and I do not enjoy all this, and particularly I do not like my job."

"Why don't you like your job?" I asked.

"This is the job my father wanted me to have. To do this job, I studied economics and accounting. I did not like these subjects, but they were very popular in my social circle. The society I belong to pushed me to go to one of the top five universities in France. I completed my studies successfully although I did not enjoy a single moment of it. I joined the largest insurance company in France. I was very ambitious. In the circles I belong to, success at work and being a top executive means a great deal and I followed this course. Here I am after more than thirty years on this journey at the very apex of my profession and I have no well-being at all. I am tired, demotivated and unhappy."

At this stage it became clear that Frederic needed some work in the East. We started exploring what really moves him as a person. This was not easy, as

Frederic was deeply disconnected from his authentic self after so many years repressing everything that really drove him from within. Frederic was the product of a life's journey driven uniquely from the outside. After a long exploration it became clear that Frederic admired beauty and art. He was deeply driven by creativity and a sense of harmony. He suppressed these tendencies at a young age because of the will of his father and the pressures of the society he belonged to. With his hobbies he tried to compensate for the fact that all those authentic drivers were missing in his work. We went deeper to understand together what these drivers and values meant for him and realized that he had a deep calling to make spaces more harmonious and more beautiful. That was his deep inner calling, which he had denied for many years. We then went into a process of connecting back to these internal drivers, like connecting to the electricity in the socket in the wall. Connecting back can be done mentally, emotionally, symbolically and in many more ways.

When Frederic felt connected again to those deeper values that drive him, we explored how he could bring these drivers into his work. Frederic remained CEO of the insurance company. He conducted a major redesign of their headquarters. He took the role of chief designer to the surprise of all his colleagues. He went on to start a fund that invested in art and in artists. The works of young artists started to appear on the walls of his offices. Later Frederic decided that his company and the employees would, from time to time, adopt institutions in poor neighborhoods that were neglected, like schools or community centers. Frederic and his employees would plan and finance redecoration and actually do the work on the weekends themselves together with the local communities. Frederic now spends less time on his yacht and less time in his vineyards, but he is a much happier and whole person. In his last email he wrote, "I am so lucky to have found ways to express my true desires and let others enjoy them as well."

East Story – Youth and values
Realizing and living in harmony with one's personal values can be complex. For people from a troubled, dysfunctional background, it can be even more challenging.

Here is a true story I heard from a Parole Officer for juvenile delinquents in the New York City Police Department.

"Trying to work with juvenile delinquents on the idea of values is almost impossible. These kids are often brought up in rough neighborhoods, dysfunctional families, and in a criminal environment. The idea of values as guiding principles is not really part of their paradigms."

"In our department, we found a marvelous way to show these kids that they do have values, and that they can live by them."

"This is what we do…"

"We ask the teenagers what they would do if we gave them one million dollars. The teenagers typically respond that, first and foremost, they would buy a fancy car. When asked what they would do with the other $900,000, a typical response is they would buy a sophisticated, expensive sound system. Then we keep on asking them what they would do with the other $890,000 and so on…"

"Usually, after they have the car, the music system, clothes, perfume, the tour around the world etc., they are still left with a huge sum of money. When we continue asking what they will do with that, we get answers like: 'I will give some to my brothers, my parents, and my friends.'"

"Now, we come to the crucial point and ask them, "Why?"."

"Often, their answers are like: 'They take care of me', 'I owe him', 'I love them', 'He's my best friend', or 'We do things together'."

"From these answers, the teenagers are shown that they are actually expressing values such as loyalty, reciprocity, honor, respect, love and so on…"

"They are usually quite surprised.

Then, we go on to help them understand these values, and how they can continue to live by them and express them in a broader way. For us, this is a great way to get true values out of the youth themselves, rather than preach to them how they should be."

The personal journey in the East has three steps:
1. Identify your "authentic drivers" and "values".
2. Better connect with them.
3. Translate your drivers and values to behaviors.

For you
Here we go into the East journey. This is a must for every person who wants to deeply connect to what motivates them, especially in situations of burnout, fatigue, auto-pilot, loss of meaning and motivation. You owe it to yourself as a human being.

THE FIRST STEP IN YOUR PERSONAL EAST JOURNEY – IDENTIFY YOUR "AUTHENTIC DRIVERS' AND VALUES

There are many ways and levels to access the personal East. Let me introduce two of the ones we use that work very well. The first one is called the '3 circles of importance'.

With this tool, you are required to identify the very few things that are most important for you in the area you wish to navigate (career, family, relations, contribution, and the like).

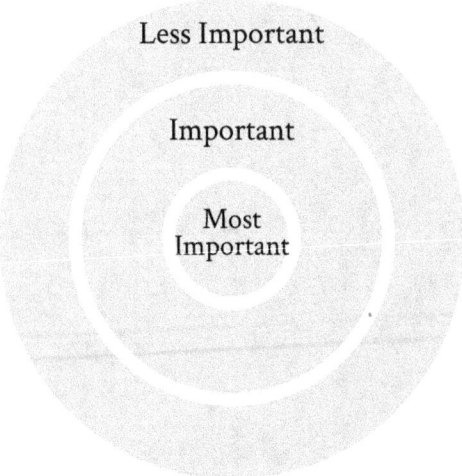

You might come up with things such as: family, working with people or creating impact. These might be at the heart of what is important for you. We can then use the second tool, which is the power of the question "Why?" "Why is that most important for you?" we can continue several times to ask "why?" each one of those is important for you. The question "Why?" creates depth.

This process is a bit like peeling an onion. After a few "Whys?", we can get as deep as the person can be conscious of, or as deep as they allow. The initial list we start with in the three circles model might in the end turn into: belonging, contribution, and creating, along with other new possibilities. The main emphasis here should be that we reach actual values and not ego needs.

A good example from a recent executive coaching that I had:

"What is most important for you?" Communication, they answered. "Why is that important?" they answered "It promotes better cooperation in the team". Why is better cooperation in the team so important? I asked. "Customers can get much better support and service".

Why is that important? "Because this is what we are here to do. It is the essence of our role".

This was a short exploration journey that started with "communication" and ended with "Customer support and service" as a reason for existence. Such a process reveals what is at the bottom of what is important for a person.

Often you will find that what is really important for a person is to be recognized, or appreciated, or other egoic needs. These are not intrinsic drivers. However, I found a wonderful way to convert that self-centeredness into understanding your hidden values.

A true story
Josh was an Australian executive in a cyber company. I coached him in his search for meaning. All his answers about what was most important for him always rotated back to himself. He did things to be recognized, to win over others and to be well paid. At one point, Josh told me that our meetings would be suspended for a month. I asked him why and he said that he was going to India for a month. I inquired why India, and Josh said that every year he volunteers for a month in a school in a deprived area and he teaches English. I asked why he does that and his answer like always was that he got a lot of appreciation and recognition from these people. And then I had a brilliant insight and it was: "Most people want to be recognized for their wealth or fame. What kind of a person would want to be appreciated for volunteering to teach English in a poor school in India?" Josh was quiet for a long time. I then asked him "What might be important for such a person who wants to

be recognized for that?" We eventually discovered together that Josh was driven by contribution and equal opportunity for people. That realization and the newly made connection to the forgotten "gems" that were in the core of his existence changed his life completely. He took this volunteering and contribution to a whole new level with this new consciousness of who he really was deep inside.

Often people will come up with drivers that are just ego based such as "recognition" or to "be known as…". As in the case of Josh, with some skilled tools, it is possible to lead others to discover the inner core values behind those ego drivers.

There is an inversion point where the outer "empty" drivers are transformed into an internal realization of what is really important.

For you
Please fill in the 3 circles diagram.

Focus mainly on the things that are most important for you. Write them down. Then ask for each of them: "Why is this important to me?".

Try to reach as deeply as you can with this questioning to discover those gems that are deep inside you.

What have you found?

Were you aware of these core drivers and values?

There are a few types of values: cultural values, wannabe values, core values.

They are dramatically different from each other. Here is a short explanation:
- Cultural values are the values you were raised with in your family, culture or religion. They are external to you and adopted from your surroundings.
- Wannabe values are values that you might be missing, that you would like to have, such as patience or inner peace, which you try to cultivate within you.
- Core values – these values are intrinsic to you because of who you are originally and authentically. They do not necessarily come from education, culture or conditioning. They are discovered as you tune into your genuine "inner voice".

Core values and core drivers have some characteristics that most people do not suspect.

1. Core values are found everywhere. This means that if a person has a core value, it will appear in all areas of their life. Let us take the value of "contribution" for example. If it is a core value for a person, it will show up in family, at work, with friends and in society. Core values cannot exist only in one segment of life. If so, they do not come from the core.

2. A core value is something you wish to see in the world. It is not something that is just for you. As an example, if you value "Respect", then you want to see more respect in the world. You appreciate its existence no matter where it is manifest. If you value respect only when it is directed at you, this is not a value. It is a demand.

3. If it is a true core value, you will be willing to pay the price for having it. You will demonstrate it in your behaviors especially in challenging situations or by respecting your standards and not compromising even when faced with social pressure or material loss. This is actually the origin of the word "Value". It has to do with price. You know a value is a true core value for you only when you are willing to pay for it. As an example, you will be willing to lose a business deal that is not in accordance with your values. Or you will be willing to leave a desired job if the codes of conduct of your manager do not align with your values. Actually, incompatibility of values often is the reason why people leave companies or managers.

While going through these criteria people sometimes realize that they do not know what their inner core values are. They discover that they are mainly driven by external drivers like appearance, popularity and success. With a few "Whys?" we can help people see a deeper part of themselves that they are not connected to.

For you
Having realized your core values, it is now time to connect more strongly to them. You might have lived disconnected to some extent from these very powerful motivators ....

SECOND STEP IN YOUR PERSONAL JOURNEY IN THE EAST – CONNECT BETTER WITH YOUR CORE VALUES.

When a person realizes what few things are most important to them, it is time to better connect to them. Those core values should be like an internal battery full of energy and drive. But for that energy to drive you, you must be connected to it. The analogy would be a car engine. The engine can be on and running, but unless you engage the gear, all that energy is just wasted potential.

There are two major ways to connect to your core drivers and values. One way is mentally. The other way is emotionally. Let's explore both. Connecting to core values mentally is done by a process of defining.

Defining what you mean exactly by that core value or driver, you connect to its deeper meaning. The process of defining is not a common practice for most people.

Drivers and Values
Why is it important to define your values?

Defining makes you fully understand what you mean by those values.

Defining values makes it easier to react appropriately and to make decisions in challenging situations.

Values are concepts without content until you fill them with your own substance. Defining values creates a structure and gives the values real significance.

Defining values allows you to coordinate expectations between you and your environment. It allows you to behave in alignment with your values in a clear manner. Because this is not a common practice, here are some guidelines to define your core values.

Guidelines for Defining Drivers and Values:

What is it?

Examples: Quality / Attribute / Ability / Feeling / Action / Essence / State of Mind / Emotion / Sensation

What is associated with the most important value? Which additional values and actions are related to it? What does it deal with?

What can it do or be? How does it manifest itself in real life? Where does it exist? (Between people, in nature, etc.)

What does it feel like?

How do you feel when you behave in alignment with this value? Your definition will be a sentence derived from the ideas above.

For you

Try to define the core values that you discovered in the previous exercise using these guidelines. Try a few times until you reach a definition that resonates.

This is neither easy nor simple if you are not trained for it. What kind of result did you get?

How was the process of defining for you?

Here, to inspire you, are some definitions created by participants in our programs. Respect - "Quality of attributing to other people and things their true value".

Care - "Ability to anticipate other's needs".

Integrity - "Being fully committed to one's principles".

Support - "Actively offering assistance to others".

Success - "Achieving your desired results".

However, the mental approach is not enough for most people. The second and better way to connect to your core values is the emotional way. Emotions connect us to things. Therefore, an emotional approach through connection was created. The questions and deliberations here are different.

For you

What is the feeling of being connected to your most important values? Can you recall a moment when you felt like this?

What is the feeling of being disconnected from your most important values? Can you recall a moment when you felt like this?

How would you symbolize your values?

Can you give an enthusiastic speech about your values and what they mean to you? This is a great exercise to do. Try and go deeply through those questions.

How did that feel?

And now you are ready for the third step in your personal deep journey in the East.

THIRD STEP IN YOUR PERSONAL JOURNEY IN THE EAST – TRANSLATE YOUR VALUES INTO BEHAVIORS.

This step is crucial. Most people live and act far from their values. This can be seen especially in challenging situations. They claim to love their spouse but do not necessarily behave like they do. They would like to be engaged parents, but sometimes in some situations, this value is hard to recognize. They might want to be cooperative colleagues at work but are often competitive and selfish.

We call this gap between values and actual behavior the "Be – Do" gap. The "Be–Do" gap is the gap between your East and your West.

It is the gap between your being and your doing.

It is the gap between your inner aspirations and your actual behavior and responses. When this gap is wide, the person lives with contradictions. They are definitely not whole. This can express itself in mental or even physical conditions.

For you
Revisit the values you found as your core values.

Choose a situation where you often do not act according to your core values at work or at home.

What behaviors do you exhibit at these times?

What happens as a result? How does this impact you? What is the impact on others?

Is that what you intend to cause, by choice? Do you want to change it?

Can you think of alternative behaviors better aligned to your core values?

To envision alternative behaviors, you need a strong imagination. Or you need a role model, a person who behaves the way you would like to, in a way you respect. They can be your inspiration and guide.

To change a behavior, you need to really want to. You need to have a very good reason for it. You need energy and/ or strong willpower and discipline to change that behavior. If you persist with this new chosen behavior for a few weeks, remembering why, it can become a new habit. It will become part of your acquired portfolio of behaviors. You will no longer need willpower or discipline. To develop a new alternative behavior, you will need to set "alarm clocks", these are reminders in various places: your desk, your computer or cell phone to remind you of the choice and decisions you have made.

This third step translates the values into behaviors and makes them real. When values are translated into behavior, they are no longer theoretical concepts and can begin to shape your life and your future reality. We live in a world where values have become very cheap. They are written on the corridors of corporations and no one pays attention to them. Politicians use values to their own ends and make them even cheaper and more meaningless.

For you
Define what drives you. Then define what you actually mean and then align your behaviors accordingly, especially in challenging situations.
This is the essence of self-leadership and navigation of the personal journey in the East.

We now invite you to take one step deeper in understanding the East journey.

PERSONAL EAST - ONE STEP DEEPER

In your journey to self-fulfillment you need to heed your inner voice. Values and intrinsic drivers are often the echo of an internal voice or compass. That internal compass can serve as your conscience. I believe we are all born unique. I believe each person has an internal universal code. Part of our mission in life's journey is to discover that inner code and give it a voice.

That will create the unique meaning of your life. In my view there is a purpose to our unique design and inherent set of values. We can make soldiers out of everyone, and many countries do. We can make waiters or guards out of everyone, no matter what they were designed for or regardless of their inner compass.

But is this the best "use" of this person? Is this the best way to spend their life on earth? Is this their highest fulfillment? Is this their best contribution to their fellow humans? Looking at ancient tribes like the aborigines of Australia it becomes evident that they had a different way. They would observe a child from a young age to understand their uniqueness. When the child grew up they would assign them their unique role in the tribe, the role where they could best contribute to the greater good, what they were born to do.

That is so simple and so beautiful, that you must ask yourself how on earth this changed and became warped over the millennia of human evolution.

Discovering, heeding, manifesting that inner voice is part of the essence of the human journey. There is no better journey to be taken than fulfilling the original potential that lies within every human being.

For you
Having completed the deep journey in the East, let us go even deeper now into your South journey. The South is hidden and often unknown. It holds the power to slow down or stop everything you attempt to do or become in your North.

THE N.E.W.S.® PERSONAL JOURNEY IN THE SOUTH

South sayings

"We don't see the world as it is, we see the world as we are." Anais Nin

"If you want to drive your car, you'd better release the handbrake before you engage the gear." Aviad Goz

The South deals with personal development and breaking through your limits. The South is the most intriguing part of the N.E.W.S.® journey. It addresses whatever is inside the individual that prevents them from expressing their full potential.

If the North is like wings that let you fly high, the South is like weights on your feet that prevent you from soaring. Internal barriers appear as fears, hesitations, concerns, lack of confidence and all their "relatives". The South exists in the realm of the psyche and is created by the stories you tell yourself about reality. The South deals with what actually stops the person from moving forward, both internally and externally.

Often there are external difficulties that are objective facts. Usually people tend to blame those external difficulties for not moving forward, for procrastinating and for not pursuing their North at full speed.

While there might be real external difficulties, what shapes the next reality is your interpretation of that difficulty. Or in other words, the story that you tell yourself about it.

The South journey is therefore concerned with your belief system, with discovering the beliefs, perceptions and stories that you uphold that stop you from achieving your goals and dreams. The South journey helps you make the decision to cross your limits with courage. Finally, the South journey is about breaking through your limits both cognitively and with actions.

The South answers the simple question "Why not?". Whenever a person wants to move forward to any destination and yet does not actually do it, the question arises "Why not?" and then "Why not now?" When you listen carefully and attentively to the sequence of answers and you continue to explore, you will eventually discover the depth of the limiting beliefs or assumptions that block progress.

At any crossroad of decision-making, the East and the South will engage in an intense dialogue. The East will voice the motivation and drive for choosing a specific course of action. The South will voice all the "Why nots", the doubts and hesitations. Eventually one of those voices will tip the scales and determine the move to be taken or not, and the subsequent reality will be determined.

Decisions driven from the East will be loyal to the inner voice or the inner compass. They may be courageous, but we accept the cost. South-driven decisions are conservative, conformist and fear-based and are deeply driven by the need for safety and security.

For you
In order to experience your South as a game, try to talk in "Gibberish" (meaningless sounds) with someone that you know and trust. Try talking Gibberish using different accents. Sense how you feel when you practice this exercise.

Most people feel embarrassed, unpleasant or even nervous when they attempt this exercise.

Why do you think most people feel like this?

The main reason is that in this exercise you usually encounter your limits. For many years, we are all educated and conditioned to be responsible, reasonable coherent adults.

We try to be clear and eloquent in our rhetoric. Our verbal system is organized to reflect the way we think and who we think we are.

To speak "Gibberish" is to cross that limit of trying to appear to be a reasonable adult. It is to cross the boundaries of language. It is not easy for most. Children would have no problem doing such an exercise.

So, what happened from childhood to adulthood?

You were conditioned with different limiting beliefs, fears, and conventions that eventually became your prison and limitation.

For you
Draw three concentric circles.

The inner one will represent the Comfort zone. The comfort zone includes actions that you are comfortable with.

The second circle will represent the Stretch zone. This circle includes actions that you will require that you stretch out of the Comfort zone in order to do them.

The outer circle will represent the Panic zone. This circle consists of those actions that the mere thought of doing them will send you into a panic response.

Imagine that you face your colleagues from work and you are asked to perform certain activities in front of them. Please write down in each circle the activities that would belong there.

Here are some examples from people I worked with for actions that they included in their stretch zone or within their panic zone. Singing in front of a group is a major one. Dancing in front of the group is number two. Giving a harsh feedback to an employee, asking for a salary raise, sharing an intimate story from your life, are all common examples.

For you
Ask yourself: Why would these activities that are so natural for human beings, cause in some people a sensation of feeling stretched or in a state of panic.

Why do the activities you noted in your panic zone evoke in you such a reaction? What are your limiting beliefs about exposing yourself in front of groups or in a social setting?

Where do these beliefs come from?

If you give thought to these exercises, you will begin to experience your South. You will experience what it might feel like when you are confronted with a limit you do not believe you can break through.

The South on the positive side is all about growth.

That's why the color that is attributed to it is green. In order to grow, you need to break out of your limitations and comfort zones.

An example from Nature:

Wherever you look in the natural world you will observe an interesting phenomenon.

As part of their life cycle most living creatures are, at some point, enclosed. They might spend some time inside an egg, in a shell, enclosed in a cocoon, a seed, a pouch or a womb. These different types of enclosures protect them and allow them to experience growth and transformation in a protected, safe environment. At some stage the living creature inside the enclosure fills it up entirely. It is then time for it to hatch, be born or break through. It might be very comfortable and cozy for the chick inside the egg. Failing to break through the shell leads to decay and even premature death.

According to biologists, approximately 80% of living creatures go through this enclosed state and break out of it as part of their life cycle. It is a mechanism that has evolved over eons and that the different species actually depend on.

We as humans also go through a stage of developing in an enclosed womb, which is called gestation. We are then born out of it. As humans we also have by way of analogy our virtual shells to grow out of. These virtual shells are the limitations and boundaries we carry in our minds. These "shell-like" limitations also offer safety and comfort. They keep us in our comfort zones, safe and secure. They eliminate the need to struggle and to break through. Like the shells in nature, the shells and barriers in our mind are both protective and limiting. Eventually if we do not break out of them at the right time, they become our prison. Sometimes we can even die inside these shells although we are still alive. These shells or prisons in our minds are constructed by us, influenced by our parents, our society and our culture.

The journey of breaking through these imposed limitations while respecting and remaining loyal to our authentic inner voice is the very essence of the human journey on earth.

So, like in nature, people also need to make breakthroughs in order to grow.

The South addresses mainly those internal barriers that hold you back from reaching your North. The South personal journey deals with levels that are often invisible and unknown. You might not even be conscious of them. And yet, they control your life and limit your freedom.

They dictate what is possible for you and what is not. It is this deep inner work that will eventually release you to reach your potential and natural greatness.

The story of Gerald, the dentist.
Gerald was the owner of a large dental clinic. There were many dentists, assistants and secretaries that worked in his clinic. I was working with Gerald on the marketing strategy of the clinic. At one point, Gerald surprised me when he suddenly said: "But I hate to come here".

"Why do you hate to come here?" I asked utterly surprised. "It is your own clinic!"

"I hate to come here because of Esmeralda, my assistant. She is so unpleasant. She makes my life and the customers' lives a living hell"

"How does she do that?" I asked

"She is really unpleasant, not service-oriented and has no patience whatsoever".

I decided to take the conversation to the South.

"So, why is she still working here?" I asked. "Why did you not send her home and replace her with another assistant?" I added.

"Because she is very professional and without her the clinic will collapse" Gerald expressed his limiting belief. "How do you know that?' I enquired.

"She was once away for a while. Someone came to replace her, and the place was in a shamble, total chaos".

"And from this single attempt you concluded that the clinic would collapse without her?' I asked.

"Yes" said Gerald "You might not understand this, but she is an expert at operating the software and the calendar of the clinic. Without her it is a big mess. But, because of her bad temper, I try to come in before she does to avoid her. I try not to run into her during the day in the corridors, and I always leave after she has gone".

"Is she your wife?" I asked just to be sure. "No. She is not." Said Gerald.

"How long has this been going on?" I asked.

"This has been going on for the last sixteen years" came the astonishing answer.

"Let me understand", I started the work in the South. "You believe that without Esmeralda the clinic will collapse. How does that make you feel?"

"It makes me feel hopeless and desperate. I suffer but I am dependent on her".
"How do these feelings make you act or behave?

"As I said" repeated the tortured Gerald. "I try to avoid her. I organize my day to avoid her. I come in first. I leave last".

"What has resulted from this so far?" I asked, "The clinic is doing well, but I really suffer".

"If this goes on in the same way for the next ten years, what kind of a reality can you envision?" I asked using a very powerful South tool.

Gerald stopped. He was thinking silently for a while, nodding his head and staring at the floor. After a long silence he suddenly erupted in a manner totally out of character and almost shouted.

"That's it. She is leaving today. I cannot bear the thought of spending ten more years like these. No way. She goes today".

"Are you sure?" I asked totally surprised again.

"Yes. She goes today. There must be someone else who can operate this software", Gerald was very firm.

And so it was. Esmeralda left that day. A week later Gerald found a nice and highly professional assistant. She was an expert on software and calendar management systems for clinics. She even brought in a more advanced version of software. She was kind and courteous to Gerald and to the patients. Gerald's life changed completely.

For you
Is there a relationship or situation in your life that you cannot change or feel you cannot get out of because of your concerns or fears?

If so, welcome to your South!

THE PERSONAL JOURNEY IN THE SOUTH - INTRODUCTION

So many people spend their lives stuck in jobs they are not suited for, that don't meet their needs or their potential, stuck with poor managers, bad marriages or miserable relationships, stuck living in the wrong place. And all of that because of limiting beliefs that prevent them from moving on and living the kind of life they are capable of. These limiting beliefs and stories keep them in prison miles away from their full potential or happiness. It is therefore crucial to try to help people break through those beliefs and stories that deprive them of their freedom and the right to pursue fulfillment and happiness.

At the basis of the development and the breakthrough of an intense South in people lies the "victim attitude". This is a deeply entrenched attitude that holds others responsible, and we blame them for our pain and suffering.

This is opposite to the "creator attitude". The Creator and Victim attitudes each have a different approach to life. They have a different language and different feelings associated with them. The Victim attitude is a typical mentality in the South. It holds a person back and prevents them from taking responsibility for their life. Though it is impossible to control everything around us, we can control how we think, feel, react and behave.

There is a very fundamental difference between the two attitudes. The victim attitude stems from fear. It leads you to abandon responsibility. It is based on an external focus of control, which means that you believe your reality is caused by external circumstances or other people. Finally, it leads to giving up on choice and personal responsibility, fundamental for navigating one's life.

To be a creator: Demonstrating the ability to initiate and take responsibility for your choices.

To be a victim: Being subject to circumstances and blaming everyone and everything else for it.

For you
Examine yourself.

In which areas of life do you have a "Creator" attitude? And in which areas of life do you have a "Victim" attitude?

You can look at your different relationships, as a spouse, as a parent, a colleague, an employee, a friend, etc.

The South personal journey sets out to overcome fears, limiting beliefs and comfort zones and above all to free you from the Victim attitude and relationships.

The personal journey in the South deals with three crucial steps:
1. Identify your "limiting beliefs": Limiting beliefs are self-imposed limitations that prevent you from achieving your North.
2. Make your choice: Crossing through your limits is always your choice and no one else's.
3. Break through your limits: Making the necessary leap, using the tools to cross through your limits into a larger space of action and freedom.

For you
Welcome to your first step in your South. It might be uncomfortable, but the rewards will be great.

FIRST STEP IN THE PERSONAL JOURNEY IN THE SOUTH – IDENTIFY YOUR LIMITING BELIEFS

Limiting beliefs can be identified by the stories you tell yourself about what is holding you back. It can be found in the narratives you carry in your mind about your reality. Often these stories or narratives are very subjective and biased and generate counter-productive behaviors.

What are the sources of South limiting beliefs?

Limiting beliefs on a personal level can originate from a variety of sources:

Education and upbringing – at a very young age, even prenatally, you are programed to perceive reality from a very particular angle. Being born in the next house, or the next city, or the next country would have completely changed your point of view. Potentially we all face the field of all possibilities. This is the space where all can happen or be created. This is what we are born into, but often we are completely unaware of this possibility. This is why we cling to the realities we create, as if they are the only ones possible for us. The field of all possibility is vast and infinite. As we grow up in a family, a society and a culture, we are conditioned in a very particular way of perceiving and therefore creating reality.

Part of our upbringing sows in us the seeds of our South.

Examples for limiting beliefs: "You are not good enough", "Girls should not do that", "In our society, you do not tell people what you really think", "All Muslims/Jews/Christians are evil", "We are born sinners" and so much more. The young mind with its hunger for learning and survival adopts such beliefs and they become the coding infrastructure for our future beliefs and attitudes. Some of this programming runs so deep that it takes great awareness and courage to break free.

Generalizing personal experience – as young children we experience various incidents. Some of them might be harsh or even traumatic. Very often people tend to generalize these harsh experiences and make them their bible of beliefs and stories. Beliefs such as: "Dogs are bad", "Having your own business is dangerous", "A person from my background cannot succeed", "Beware of priests. They are all child molesters", "Never swim against the social currents", "Be pretty and and shut up", and so much more.

You can easily guess what kind of experiences led to these limiting beliefs. Generalizing experiences and making them into a belief system is one way in which the South is created.

Common, shared cultural beliefs, distorted information and Fake news. Even if we grew up as what is determined loosely as "normal human beings", we find ourselves in groups, workplaces, societies and organizations. Each of these has its own South, which will impact you if you fail to conform. Beliefs such as "Management does not care about us", "We tried it before and it never worked", "The market is very tough now", "Competition is too strong", "Be careful who you share your ideas with".

These group beliefs are contagious. We may not even be aware of their long-term impact.

The "Shadow of Greatness" – This source of South beliefs is a bit more complex to explain.

People have their unique natural greatness, which has a range of expression from high to low. The lower part of a person's greatness is a natural limit that they need to cross in their journey towards free choice and fulfillment.

Here are a few examples I encountered working with different people.

One person might be great with details. The lower part of that gift is a tendency to be pedantic. To use that talent for details in a constructive way, the person will have to overcome that "shadow".

A person might be very creative. The lower aspect of that can be disorganization or dispersion. To express their creativity to the world, the person will have to cross through chaos and create a certain degree of order, although in most cases they would not enjoy the process at all.

Another person might be excellent in planning. The "shadow" of that greatness might appear as over-planning, control and refraining from any action or any move before everything is perfectly planned. This can prevent a person from attaining many achievements, as they always wait to have the perfect plan. Eventually if they do not go through that natural barrier, they might be sitting at home, doing nothing, waiting for some perfect plan or for some ultimate readiness.

All talents and gifts have their shadow side. That shadow translates into tendencies and beliefs that the person needs to overcome in order to express their greatness.

For you
Time to start our journey in the South. Brace yourself as we are going to dive deeply into what might have held you back for long time.

STEP ONE IN YOUR PERSONAL JOURNEY IN THE SOUTH IDENTIFYING YOUR LIMITING BELIEFS

The identification of your South is by way of analogy much like peeling an onion. You can go in deeper and deeper. You can go as deeply as your consciousness allows. The leading question in this identification process is – WHY NOT?

For you
To illustrate this, please review the North you created earlier and ask yourself "So, why haven't I done this?"

"Why not now?"

"Why not full steam ahead?"

From your responses you can explore deeper and deeper the main reason or belief that is currently preventing you from achieving your full potential.

What we look for is a "bug" in the system. We look for a narrative or a notion that is at the core of what you tell yourself that prevents you from taking action and moving forward.

Narratives Such as:

"I will lose my job, if I tell them what I really think".

"I cannot do it because my family may not have the lifestyle that they want".

"If I go for what I want no one will appreciate me".

We do not look for a description of a phenomena such as "Fear of rejection" or "fear of failure".

We look for the actual story that we tell ourselves that holds us back.

For you

To understand this more clearly, choose one of your dreams that you have not yet fulfilled. Ask yourself:

"Why have I not fulfilled this dream?" "Why have I not done anything sooner?"

If you keep asking yourself these questions, you will discover your limiting belief that prohibits you from fulfilling that dream.

There are many supportive questions that can help explore your South. Such as: What external causes are stopping me from achieving my North?

What internal causes are stopping me from achieving my North?

What are the stories I tell myself that stop me from achieving my desired result?

As you explore this unknown territory, you may find many barriers and limiting beliefs.

You need to concentrate only on those that are blocking you on the journey to your North.

Exploring all limiting beliefs and their origins, is therapy.

This is definitely not our intention. As you might find many barriers, concentrate only on the most significant ones that seem the most limiting in your journey to fulfillment.

In the South when relating to a relevant topic, people have in the back of their mind what can be described as "The worst-case scenario". This is an imaginative series of events that would lead to what the person fears most.

Here is an example of a dialogue with a senior executive in a multinational pharmaceutical company who was unable to tell his boss his opinion of the organization's strategy:

Me: "Why won't you tell your boss your opinion?"

Executive: "He won't like it".

Me: "So what?".

Executive: "He will become antagonistic towards me".

Me: "So, what might happen?".

Executive: "I might lose my job".

Me: "So what? You are talented. You are well known in the industry. You can easily find another job".

Executive: "Well, you know, I have a family to look after. I can't just lose a job and hope that all will be well".

Me: "But surely with the right preparation you can find another job, no?"

Executive: "No. I might end up like my father".

Me: "What happened to your father?"

Executive: "He lost his job when he was 45 and he sat at home drinking himself to death. This can't happen to me".

This executive would not tell the CEO his opinion about the strategy of the organization because deep in his mind the worst-case scenario is that he would end up like his father. To allow your fears to run your life is never a good idea. It is actually the worst place to operate from. It never leads anywhere good. Experience proves this again and again. Other people around you sense your fears consciously or even subconsciously. The relationship between you and those people will be heavily impacted.

When your fears are the foundation for your relationships, you will be used, exploited or even abused. Unnecessary dependencies will evolve, and you will be stuck without much hope of getting ahead. Relationships between people are often like a default structure that is built between them. Wherever the structure is based on fear, the relationship will become painful or full of suffering. This is another reason to take the journey in the personal South. In an almost magical way, when you overcome a limiting belief or a fear that is a basis for your relationship with another person, they sense it immediately, even if it happens only in your mind.

They will sense that something has changed, and they react to that, even without your having to do or say anything, they will respond to your change in attitude. I have seen this happen so many times to people who conquered their fears.

The executive discussed above overcame his fear. He shared his thoughts with the CEO. A year later he was promoted.

For you
Let me introduce to you a very powerful tool that I developed for the South journey. It is called the "Diamond Model."

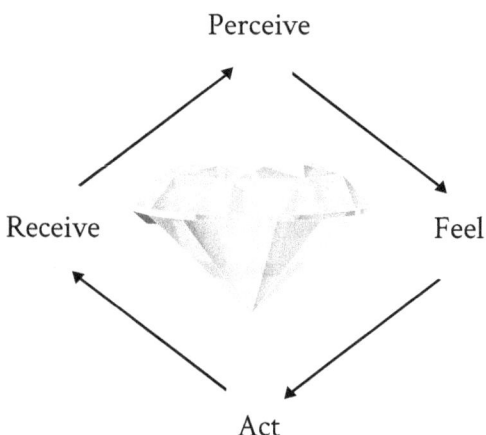

The Diamond Model is a powerful tool in the South that demonstrates how your perceptions create your reality and how you can change your reality by changing your perceptions. The reason I created the model was to help people understand that the way they view reality is just one option among many others. I knew that to change their perceptions, people need to understand that their strong view is a mere perception that can be changed if needed. Let us start at the top.

Perceive - Different people perceive reality differently. Two people looking at the same reality will have a different perception about it. For example: person A might think "This direction is unsafe", while person B will think "What an adventure it must be to go in this direction!"

Person A might think: "We need to work hard to succeed", while person B might think "We can take it easy and enjoy".

Person A might think "Never trust your employees", and person B working next to them might think "The only way to get ahead is to empower our employees."

Perceptions are the way people view reality. They are the translations of reality on a personal level. In the words of Anais Nin "People do not see reality as it is. They see it as they are".

The question might arise then: "Who is right?" This kind of deliberation will lead to arguments, conflict or wars. The sad truth is that most people are absolutely convinced that the way they view reality is the only right way to view it. This has led to endless human made conflicts and tragedies throughout history. Therefore, the only thing I can say about this with any degree of certainty is that different people view reality differently. Because they see things differently, they experience different feelings about them.

Feel – Different perceptions evoke specific feelings in people such as fear, frustration, anger, happiness. These feelings create a certain state that eventually will lead them to take certain actions. Let's take an example: If you think there is no one on your team you can really trust, how will this make you feel? You will feel alone, frustrated, with the responsibility for everything on your shoulders.

Act – Those feelings drive us to act in certain ways and adopt specific types of behavior.

To continue our example above: That feeling of being alone and frustrated will lead you to act independently. You will do most of the work yourself, you will not delegate. You will be busy all day long. This behavior will generate certain results.

Receive - These feeling, actions and behaviors eventually lead you to receive certain results. These results will most likely reinforce your original beliefs, thus creating a vicious cycle. In our example the results of doing everything alone and not delegating to others will probably lead to a whole set of results both for you and the people around you. Results for you such as fatigue, burnout and demotivation. People around you will not develop or grow, will get stuck and do very little. Finally, you will tell yourself "I knew it from the beginning, there is no one here I can trust."

This is how the vicious circle is created and how reality gets recycled again and again. This cycle will become permanent and fixed.

Let us take another example from the family arena:

Perceive – "I have to give my children everything, so that they will not have to struggle like I did."

Feel – When dealing with my children I feel protective. I feel that I need to cover up for them, forgive them, provide endlessly for them. I will even feel guilty when I do not spoil them.

Act – I will spoil my children. I will not demand anything from them. I will respond to their whims. I will give them too many games, too many clothes, too much of everything.

Receive – As a result I will probably create very spoiled children. Their demands will probably grow exponentially. Then I will find myself worried, feeling guilty and deeply dissatisfied.

In this way, "You create your reality". This is not a perception that most people hold. Most would assume that reality is a given that they operate within. That they are subject to it. In the spirit of the "Diamond Model", I would like to invite you to consider the idea that we create our reality by the way we perceive it, feel about it, and act upon it. Our "raw materials" for creating our reality are factors like where we were born, our gender, nationality, religion, decade in which we were born, etc. But this is only that - raw materials from which we can create our reality. Different people therefore will create absolutely different realities from very similar raw materials. A person with a strong "can do" attitude might have a very difficult starting point but will create a very prosperous successful reality. Another person with a "can't do" attitude might be born into a very fortunate context but might end their life miserably.

As the old saying goes "It does not matter if you have a spoon or a bulldozer, the only question is how much are you willing to dig". Some people escape from prison using a spoon and some people who own a bulldozer might leave it parked in their backyard.

When viewing things from the North perspective there are limiting beliefs and supportive beliefs. Supportive beliefs are those that help you attain your North. Limiting beliefs are those that stop you or slow you down to get to where you want.

A limiting belief - "If I attempt this move, I will surely fail."

A promoting belief - "I can learn from each failure."

Limiting and promoting beliefs define the reality you create.

Changing reality
According to the "Diamond Model", you are motivated to change things when you don't receive the results that you expected. Usually if you aren't happy with results, you change your actions or behaviors. As an example, when you

are not happy with your weight, you go on a diet or start sports. Everyone who has ever tried to change results by changing their behavior knows how difficult that is. You have behavioral habits that you have created over years. These habits die hard. Simply changing the behavior without changing the belief that gave rise to that behavior, is like changing an application while keeping the same operating system. In truth, nothing really changes. The only way to change results through behavior is to apply tremendous self-discipline and willpower. As an example, people who start going to the gym and through self-discipline and tenacity create, step by step, a new set of habits that persists over time. The other way to change through behavior is when a person is under external discipline or pressure, like in the army or in a prison. In those situations, people may change behaviors and habits. So, discipline either internal or external must be involved.

The only way to change your results and probably your life in a sustainable long-term manner is by changing your operating system. This means changing your belief system and perceptions. When that happens, feelings change. Then behaviors change much easier and new results appear.

There are two distinct ways to change your perceptions and shift into new paradigms.

The first one is through a life-changing event. That event can be a trauma, a death, an accident, or a sudden change in the circumstances that force you to review your beliefs. This kind of event is specific and conscious. The ancient Chinese used to call this kind of change – a frog leap. The second way you can shift your perceptions and change is slow and gradual. This process happens over time by reflecting, meaningful conversations, watching movies, reading books, attending lectures, going through a meaningful coaching, therapy or any intensive personal development work. In this case it may be difficult to pinpoint when your perception actually changed. There is no specific point in time. This is a process of maturing over time. The ancient Chinese called this type of change in perception the slow move of a turtle. Eventually changes and shifts in perception happen by the way of the frog or by the way of a turtle.

For you
Think about a time in your life when your perception about something changed.
Can you remember what provoked that change?
Can you remember what you realized or perceived?
Can you remember how that change of perception influenced your life from that time onwards?

Some of your beliefs are limiting and blocking. Some of your beliefs prompt you to achieve what you really want.

To give up on a limiting belief is a bit like going through eye surgery to remove glasses that are attached to your head. It is not easy.

For you
Let us now dive into what might be your limiting beliefs.
It is for you to discover. Let me lead you with some questions. Try to answer candidly.
What stops you from achieving your North? What stops you from getting there faster?
What is the worst thing that might happen if you go for your North? What is the problem with that?
So, why not?

Note – It is always better to conduct this inquiry with a skilled N.E.W.S.® coach.

For you
As a result of this self- inquiry, some sentences, narratives, stories you tell yourself, which you perceive as objective reality may arise. And yet they are the perception of reality in your mind.
Finally choose the one that seems most limiting. Write it down and keep it with you.
Congratulations, you have completed the first step in personal South. That was a challenging task.
Welcome now to the second step in the South. Your ability to choose.

STEP TWO IN THE PERSONAL SOUTH JOURNEY: MAKE YOUR CHOICE.

Crossing through your limits is always your choice and no one else's.

We must choose to break through our South. This involves costs we may not want to pay.

The price to be paid, whether imaginary or real, is what stops most people from choosing to break through their self-imposed limits. Often these prices are only in their mind and have nothing to do with reality.

This is something to be explored and worked out with a coach.

To help people make that choice we use the Diamond Model™ which is part of the N.E.W.S.® proprietary toolset.

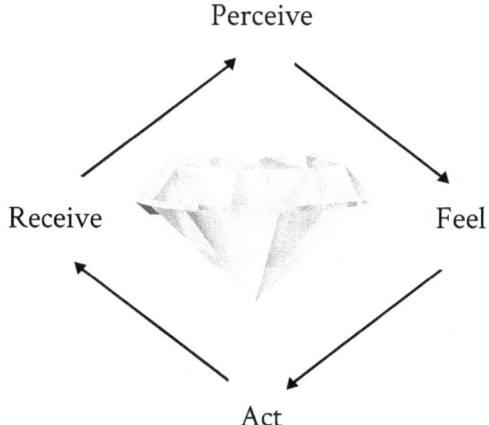

Here is the process to help you with that choice:

For you
Please take the most limiting belief you have discovered and incorporate it into the model at the level of "perceive".
My main "limiting belief" in achieving my North is...
How does this belief make me feel in relevant circumstances? How does this belief make me act in these circumstances?
What results has this created for me in the past few years?
If I carry on with this belief in the next 5- 10 years, what results will it give me? Where will it take me?
Will I be able to achieve my practical vision in the North? If not, do I want to do something about it?
Am I willing to pay the price?

This sequence of questioning will bring you to a point of choice. Remember Gerald, the dentist? It was this line of questioning and challenging that brought him to a point where he could choose to stop his unfortunate relationship with his assistant Esmeralda after sixteen terrible years.

It seems that people can bear almost anything from one day to the next. But when faced with the "critical mass" of what this might mean for the next five to ten years, they realize the impact. This "critical mass" allows them to make choices, sometimes after many years of hesitating, procrastinating and suffering. N.E.W.S.® coaches around the world use this methodology and have released thousands of people from various "stuck" situations.

In a meeting with thirty such coaches a few years ago, each of them was asked to summarize the result of a coaching process with one of their coachees in one sentence. The following are examples:

"She finally decided to go for her dream and open her business."

"He moved on to a new career path after many years."

"She stopped going out with the group she no longer liked and created new friendships."

"He retired from his boring job and started doing gardening which he has always loved."

"She finally broke the relationship with her abusive friend and found new love."

Hearing such stories from thirty experienced coaches was a very powerful experience. Most of these happened due to a breakthrough in the South. Breaking through the South depends on choice. There is an energy that is needed to make such a move. It is a bit like gathering energy for a high jump. Sometimes that energy can come from a supportive friend or a coach. Breaking through the South also releases energy.

For you
If you have made your choice, you are now invited to actually go beyond your limit. Do you have the energy to do that?

Do you need support from someone else? Can you ask them?

It may not be as difficult as you might think.

STEP THREE IN PERSONAL SOUTH JOURNEY - BREAK THROUGH YOUR LIMITS

After making a choice to break through a limiting belief, it is yet to be done. There are a few tools to help you cross your limits into a larger space of action and freedom. Many indigenous cultures have initiation ceremonies and rites of passage for this kind of breakthrough. Many methods were established over the years to assist people to overcome their limits. Some are cognitive. Some are emotional. Some are logical, some practical, some emotional and some are ceremonial. Different methods are suitable for different people at different times and different circumstances. Here is a list of nine different ways to break through your South once you have chosen to do so.

1. Examine its current relevance.
2. Redefine.
3. Small breakthroughs - "baby steps".
4. "Double S".
5. "Rituals".
6. Rewriting - creating an alternative statement.
7. Getting energy and support from others.
8. Guided imagination.
9. Practice/rehearsal.

For you
Let's look into some of those methods. You can then choose the one that suits you best.

The Cognitive Approach
Examine relevance – The initial place to start is with your perception. Changing perception will create great impact. It needs to be real, genuine

and deep. In this approach, the person checks the relevance of the belief - Is it really true? Is it always true? Is there any evidence? Where was it learned? Like an attorney litigating in court, the truth of the limiting belief is sometimes broken down. Then you can understand that it is only a false story you tell yourself. This approach is mostly useful with logical people who have a good degree of self-awareness. As an example, a person might think that they are not doing well financially. It is sometimes easy to present evidence of their situation economically in comparison with the average world population. Someone who believes they don't have enough time for a specific activity can easily be shown that they do if they allocate specific time slots.

Redefine – Sometimes redefining what something actually means helps people to change their view and understanding about that topic and cross their South.

As an example, a person who needs to ask for payment for their services might think it is not respectful (strange ah?). They need a whole redefinition about money, about creating value. About exchanging value for money, etc. Someone else might think they are not successful. In some cases, they will need to redefine what success is for them.

Redefining works beautifully if you engage terms like "Who said? Or "Where is it written?"

Rewriting Beliefs – This method creates new promoting beliefs which, when repeated, can replace the old limiting beliefs.

This method comes from neuroscience. Repetitive beliefs or ways of thinking create strong links between different neuronal centers in the brain. These links become a default network that responds automatically to different situations and stimuli. This default network cannot be erased, because it is embedded in our neuronal system. The only way is to go around it is to create new connections that, will create a bypass to the automatic established response. This is done by repetition of the new belief about the same topic. When repeated it will become a viable option for the neuronal "traffic" in the brain. It is like walking across a field that no one has ever gone through whilst bypassing an established parallel path to create a new path to cross a field. When repeated many times, this new path becomes established so that it becomes an alternative option to the original path. This is called "creating a lateral thinking pathway."

The alternative belief must not be the opposite of the limiting belief, as the unconscious mind will reject it. It needs to be perceived as logical. It needs to be gradual, proactive and positive. It needs to be short and formulated in the present tense.

Practical Methods
Changing your mind about something is not enough. It needs to be followed up with concrete actions in the material world. Otherwise it fades and has no material appearance in reality. It is my belief and experience that only one of them, (mind or practical) cognition or action alone, is not enough to create real lasting change. Beliefs that simply invite reality to happen do not usually materialize. Working in the material reality without envisioning where you will go, will also not take you very far.

Baby Steps – Finding a few small new actions you can take in the near future. These new actions should be outside your comfort zone. They will expand your freedom beyond the current limit. The steps should be small so you can succeed easily, like a baby learning to walk. They should be inspired by your alternative belief, mentioned before.

Josie could not exercise. In her mind, to exercise properly meant running at least 10,000 meters. So, she did nothing. After a conversation with her, she agreed to redefine what exercising meant. It now meant "any physical activity that is out of my comfort zone". The first baby step she took, was to walk around her block every day. This was approximately 200 meters. A week later she walked around four blocks. This was already 800 meters each time. Two weeks later she walked more than 1000 meters four times a week. To cut a long story short, after six months Josie ran 10,000 meters for the first time, to her great delight and her family's astonishment.

"Double S" – Building the next phase and its infrastructure while completing the current phase in order to ensure a seamless transition in the future. This tool is highly effective when making significant changes, like changing a role or a career. That kind of transition often evokes deep South fears.

Walter was an HR manager in a company. The job was good, the salary was ok. But Walter felt that he could do more. His passion was to become an independent organizational coach. However, this independent career was not financially safe. So, Walter delayed this move for years and his South became insurmountable. Until he learned about the concept of the Double S. Following this method, he continued with his HR job and at the same time, took a coaching certification program twice a week in the evenings. After a year he was certified as a coach.

He started coaching 2-3 people pro bono to gain experience. By word of mouth Walter gained popularity. When he had five people that were waiting to be coached by him and were willing to pay, Walter left his HR job and landed safely in his new career and got off to a very promising start.

There are some emotional and even ritualistic ways to go beyond your South. They involve ceremonial departure from South chains, sometimes even in public.

For you
I would recommend a combination of two different ways. One cognitive, and the other practical, which together are very effective. Modern practice sometimes calls this combination "Cognitive – Behavioral" approach. This will be the combination of "Writing an alternative belief" together with "Baby steps".
Let's go a bit deeper into these two methods combined.

When creating an alternative belief to your own limiting belief, there are a few important guidelines to take into consideration.

Guidelines for writing an alternative belief.
A brief sentence with a maximum of eight to ten words. The sentence must carry a positive meaning.

The sentence should be in the present tense.

"Keep it realistic"; it must fit with the facts of the existing situation. The sentence must sound right and make you feel comfortable.

The sentence needs to be proactive and offer gradual progress.

We recommend that you use words or expressions and add an explanation why:

"I deserve to…"

"I am capable of…"

"I have the right to…" "It is possible to …"

For you
As an interesting exercise, try to work out the original limiting belief of those alternative belief statements.

"I deserve to have my own time, once in a while".

"In every situation there is something useful".

"I can carefully start a new initiative".

"I can begin to get help from others".

"Other people can sometimes do some things well".

For you
Try to work out your alternative belief sentence.

Try a few versions and then choose the one that you resonate most with. Then repeat it to yourself in different ways many times every day for at least a month.

"Baby steps"
There are criteria for a "baby step". It needs to be:
- Very practical
- In the light of your new alternative belief
- Specific
- Beyond your current limit

"Baby steps" are new behaviors that express the new belief. They must be small and careful to ensure success. These "Baby steps", if done well, allow a person to cross a huge barrier in their mind in a gradual and feasible way. "Baby Steps "are a West- bound solution, as they move into practicality and implementation. Succeeding with "Baby steps" creates a feedback loop with the new alternative belief. The process is empowering and accelerates the speed of change. Let me emphasize again, to use only one of these techniques will prove futile. You must change the operating system and the application at the same time. Both together strengthen and amplify each another. The realm of the mind is creative, and the realm of practicality is where creativity needs to manifest to move beyond simply good intentions.

For you

What would your "baby steps" be in light of your alternative belief? When will you start them?

This concludes your three-step personal journey in the South. Either you continue on your own or choose to work with a coach to go further. This is a journey that can lead to profound transformation in your life and career.

You are invited now to take one step deeper.

PERSONAL SOUTH - ONE STEP DEEPER

Just as we are born with our unique inner voice, we were also born with our unique boundaries that we need to cross through in our journey. Our Greatness alludes to what is the shadow that we need to cross. When we are conceived, we face a field of endless possibilities.

Through education we become wired by family, culture, society, and the possibilities shrink. We begin to see a very narrow version of reality. We are coded like software to perceive reality in a very particular way. We are also told very often that this way of reality that we inherited is true and therefore the only way. With this kind of indoctrination and conditioning come separation, distrust of differences, conflict, struggles, and even war. It is only when you begin to question your own computation and belief system, that you can start your independent journey to a life of meaning and fulfillment. It is therefore wise to question your inherited beliefs. I have been doubting mine intensely for years. It is wise to understand where these beliefs take you and whether they help you create the kind of life you want and are entitled to. In my mind every human being is entitled to have a life of Fulfillment, Joy, Contribution and Love.

Humanity is not doing a very good job of allowing this to happen. There is too much separation. There are too many extremists. A lot of progressive ideas at the end of the 20th century are now at risk. The financial crisis of 2008 threw many people back into the arms of disbelief and distrust. Many people feel they were pushed back in the "queue for opportunity" because of immigration, minorities and so on. These phenomena significantly increase the tendency toward nationalism, or even racism and xenophobia. Perhaps all this revival of separatist ideology is here to remind us again how wrong things can go.

Or it may be that the human species is simply a species prone to war and conflict. I have spent my entire life creating consensus and peace among different people.

I sincerely hope that this perception that the human race is inherently a fighting species is wrong and that there is a place for further hope for the future.

For you
After going through the South journey and breaking through some limits, it is time to become very practical. Welcome to your personal West journey.

YOUR PERSONAL JOURNEY IN THE WEST

The Story of Noel the writer

Noel was a brilliant writer. He published a number of books and they became bestsellers in their field. Following that, he became a public figure and people would even recognize him in the street or in shopping centers.

It seemed that life was shining upon Noel and that Fortuna, the goddess of luck, favored him above others. We were therefore surprised when we got a request to coach Noel.

It turned out that Noel was extremely disorganized. He was a genius in his writing, but not in the way he was managing himself. Noel was always late for meetings, and late with any delivery date and any assignment he took on. Noel never knew where he put his things. His computer was a total mess. Worse, Noel couldn't find anything. He didn't have a filing system. He didn't have a calendar. He didn't have goals or even a simple "to do" list, not even on a napkin. He actually objected to the idea of bringing order to the chaos he was living in. It was his ideology in a way, that in order to create you need total chaos. The reason we were called to coach Noel was because he lost the draft of his next book that he had been working on for the past two years.

Of course, Noel didn't have a backup of the manuscript. He didn't know where he stored it, or even if he had. When we met him, he was broken, "Two years of my life were wasted" he said in an agonized voice. "It was supposed to be my best book ever. Now it is gone. There is no way I will write it again. That's it. I am quitting. This is too much to bear".

It was not easy to see the famous writer in this miserable condition. Before getting started, we defined our approach. We knew that people can be champions and geniuses in one area and really weak in other areas. Our philosophy of coaching has always been: "Develop people in their areas of strength, because there, they can be world champions and contributors". The other aspect of it was: "in their weak areas people need to be strengthened. They will never be champions in those areas, but these "weak muscles" should be developed to a reasonable level. Otherwise these weak areas will endanger the strengths and possibly cause the "whole ship to sink". That is exactly what happened to poor Noel.

So, we began by discussing chaos and order. We agreed that creativity often comes out of chaos. We also agreed that some measure of order is required to bring creativity to fruition. Practically speaking, we started by setting critical goals. This way of thinking was strange for Noel. However, because his situation was critical and desperate, he finally agreed to this idea. The critical goals were supposed to focus Noel on what was critical to succeed with his new book. We made some progress. Then we started discussing 20/ 80 weekly activities. This was more challenging. The idea of blocking time slots in advance for specific activities was really out of Noel's scope. He especially resisted the idea of setting time for creative work. He said "I write when I have the muse to write. How can I plan this? It is impossible". We asked, "Where do you write best?". Noel thought a bit and said, "Sitting on a hill above the sea gives me a lot of inspiration".

"So, if we organize that twice a week you take a little cabin in the hills above the sea not far from here, will that help?"

"Of course," smiled Noel. He loved the idea. "You know" we said. "You will need to book this place in advance for specific times".

"Oh" said Noel "That is not a problem at all". So, Noel started having regular times and a regular place to create, and rewriting the lost book started to advance very well.

In one area, however, it was impossible to coach Noel. That area was organizing his papers and computer files. He just could not do that. He tried again and again and could not sustain it over time. We agreed on a workaround solution. When a person cannot overcome a particular issue, we get another person to help them out. We call that a bypass. The individual does not develop skills but finds a short-cut - assistance. We found Alexandra, a young literature student who wanted writing lessons from Noel. In exchange she agreed that she would come over once a week and organize his papers and computer files. This was a win-win agreement and it worked. They both benefited.

The best part was that after a while, Alexandra found the file of the lost book buried somewhere deep in the bowels of the computer. Noel's new book was published a few months later with the new additions and was an immediate success.

YOUR PERSONAL JOURNEY IN THE WEST
INTRODUCTION

The journey in the West is one of planning and execution. The question in the West is "How to achieve the North?". For many people, the West is challenging. It can be a cultural issue, or lack of education in life skills, or lack of discipline, or even the absence of a personal inclination towards order and planning. The main challenge in the West is keeping long-term strategic focus while going through the daily "tornado" of activities, messages, crises and so on. Many people are so overwhelmed and over-burdened with all these distractions that they give up planning altogether. They just respond to events and crises as they occur.

The ability to operate well in the West depends on a few capabilities:

The ability to see the bigger, fuller picture.

The ability to break it down into its elements.

The ability to see the sequence of how these elements and actions should be organized.

The ability to perceive timeframes.

All these capabilities, with a good level of self-discipline, constitute what it takes to be able to develop a strong, tactical, results-oriented West.

The West has two parts: Planning and Execution.

The planning part occurs before getting started, and requires understanding everything needed for the task to be accomplished. Only then can a person create a plan that takes into account the time, resources and even people needed.

Execution requires a certain amount of discipline and perseverance. These virtues are apparently rare. So, many people need some type of external accountability system, or other people, that obliges them to do what they have taken upon themselves to do.

There are three steps in the Planning part of the Personal West:
1. Defining "critical goals": To focus there is a need to identify the very few goals that will make a real difference.
2. Creating a "tactical plan": Set the needed steps and timelines to achieve the goals.
3. Set a "weekly focus": Have a weekly process that focuses on the necessary actions to advance the plans.

These three steps will ensure progress toward long-term vision and goals despite the tornado of daily events.

For you
Here are a few very simple steps you can adopt and use, if you so choose.

Welcome to your first step in the West, applying an orderly way to achieve what you really want.

FIRST STEP IN THE PERSONAL WEST DEFINING CRITICAL YEARLY GOALS

Goal- setting has been around forever. Although it is an ancient methodology that was revived some 50 years ago as the MBO system (Management by Objectives), it is still as effective as it always has been.

The Importance of Setting Goals is obvious. Goals create focus.

Focus - When you set very few specific goals to achieve, it creates focus amongst the endless other things that go on, need to be done, and all the other noise around.

Commitment – When goals are known and agreed to, people are much more committed.

Motivation – Setting goals creates motivation. It appeals to the competitive and the winning instinct in people and drives some of them to achieve them.

Sense of achievement and satisfaction – Most roles involve a lot of routine work. Setting goals sets the bar for measuring success in routine jobs, as well. When you start to measure performance based on goals, people experience achievement and satisfaction. Simply doing routine work with no measures for success will result invariably in demotivation and disengagement.

Pygmalion effect – Self-fulfilling prophecies. When you know exactly what you want to achieve, your chances of achieving it improve.

There are two types of Goals:
1. Critical goals - People may have many goals but only a few are critical. Critical goals are the goals that make a significant difference when achieved at a given time. Critical goals come out of long-term goals or vision and are crucial to achieve on the way to the long-term vision. If these critical goals are not achieved no other achievement will be significant.
   Critical goals must be:

- Strategic - at the very heart of what will take you to your future.
- In your sphere of influence - where you can influence and achieve results.
- Feasible- as they relate to a year or a quarter, they need to be realistic and practical.
- The most productive: 20/80 – The few goals that lead to most of the needed impact.
- Essential - if these goals are not identified and achieved, nothing else matters.
  These are the goals that you want to focus on at any given time before you focus on other types of goals.

2. Important goals - Goals with considerable impact in terms of results or value.

For you
Review the three-year vision you created in the North.

What must be achieved in the coming year in order to reach your vision? List at least 5-7 goals. That will be your long list.

Choose the 3 most critical goals. Those will be your shortlist. Now set the indicators and measurements of success.

Defining the few most critical goals at any time is the first step to make you highly focused.

Welcome now to the second step, which is even more practical.

SECOND STEP IN THE PERSONAL WEST - CREATE YOUR TACTICAL PLAN

When you have the annual critical goals, the next step is to develop a plan to achieve them. There are many different ways to develop tactical plans. Tactical – from ancient Greek – organizing into practicality.

One of the easiest ways to do this is by writing down the goal in the middle of a page or diagram, and writing down around it everything that will be needed to achieve the goal: resources, activities, people etc.

Then determine the level of importance of each of these elements.

You can choose three levels of importance - Must/Critical, Important or they might be just Nice to have.

This is a process of prioritization. Those elements that are a must, or critical should be arranged on a timeline.

The timeline can be arranged by months or by quarters. So, what you end up with is a plan of activities by months or quarters. All these activities should be arranged in one place or one file so that you can access them frequently. Most people do not do this on a regular basis. They might plan in this way only for an important event like a wedding, for example. They plan and organize it well because of its significance and because of the terrible consequences if it is not organized properly. For some reason they fail to apply this in their daily life. This means that they have the capacity but not the mindset to operate it regularly.

This simple methodology works and maintains long-term focus in the midst of the many unplanned happenings.

For you
Try to create your own plan to achieve your critical goals in the coming year. Welcome to the third step in the West, which is a focus tool for the short-term.

THIRD STEP IN THE PERSONAL WEST- SET A "WEEKLY FOCUS"

This tool is very simple and very powerful. The idea is to have a weekly process that focuses on the necessary activities to advance long-term goals and plans. The simple version of this is to take time once a week near the weekend. This is better done sitting for few minutes in a quiet place.

First, review your vision and yearly goals. This is much like climbing from the jungle floor to a treetop. This gives you a long-term perspective instead of just running on the jungle floor and getting lost."

After reviewing the vision and goals, think about the few key activities that will advance you towards the long-term goals in the following week. We call them 20/80 activities according to the Pareto principal. Vilfredo Pareto was an Italian economist. He was hired by the Italian government in the 18th century to try to improve tax collection. He discovered that 20% of landowners owned 80% of the land. These were the rich nobles and estate owners. He found that 80% of the population owned 20% of the land. These were the poor peasants and farmers. Pareto reported to the government that they should focus their tax collection on the 20% that own 80% of the land. And thus, the Pareto principle was born. It is used in many areas to distinguish that 80% of results come from 20% of efforts, clients etc.

The 20/80 activities are those few activities that create the greatest impact in the coming week. They should be very specific. For example, calling someone or scheduling a meeting. Those activities can be put in the calendar with a specific time to do them. If it is not possible to put the activity in the calendar, it is not really an activity, but rather a nice idea or intention.

After choosing those few activities, they need to be scheduled. This means allocating a specific time for them in the calendar in advance. If not, they will fade away like many other good intentions. After scheduling those 20/ 80 activities for the following week it is time for you to commit. Unfortunately, most people commit better to other people than to themselves. It is therefore a good idea to leverage this and commit to someone else. If there is a meeting that was set with someone else at a specific time and location, in most cases it will probably happen. If people promise to send a report to someone else by Thursday, they will probably do it. The 20/80 weekly activities tool is a bi-focal view of looking far into the future and from that perspective looking at the coming week to program future-based activities. This approach instills a habit of progression towards long-term goals and vision, particularly in those areas that are most important. This helps us move from current only activities and firefighting into "Future – based" activities. And allows you to build the future and avoid drowning in minor, currently pressing activities.

For you

Please review your long- term goals and vision. Please set 4-5 activities that can be accomplished next week "to move the needle" in the direction of what you want to achieve in the future.

Please set them in your calendar. Commit to doing them.

Respect your commitment and "just do it." How do you feel when you manage to do that? You are now invited to explore a deeper step.

PERSONAL WEST - ONE STEP DEEPER

The struggle in the West is to bring order into chaos. When you understand astrophysics, you realize that the natural state of things is entropy. This means that everything in the universe tends to expand and move out of its center. This is how more and more chaos is created. In order to create order, there needs to be an investment of energy on an ongoing basis. Only this constant investment will maintain order and allow you to choose the type of order or pattern you want to create. We all function in set patterns defined and governed by the state, society, laws, or the workplace. All these patterns respect and maintain a certain order. It is very much like the matrix in the famous movie of the same name. Within all that, you can create your own order and your own patterns, so that you can lead the life that you want. To do that you will need a set of principles. You will need a clear set of priorities. You will need to decide what is really important for you and what you place at the center of your life. You will also need to identify those things or people that lie outside your center of importance. A good way to do this is to use the 3-circles model described in the East journey. Your life is yours to create, and you create it by setting the patterns and structures of what is important for you. This might include your belief system, your emotions, your feelings and your relationships.

Freedom comes with discipline. She who wants to freely improvise on a piano needs many years of disciplined practice beforehand. He who wants to dance gracefully and freely, should have a disciplined journey of exercise and a strict diet for many years to be able to do that.

Malcolm Gladwell in his extraordinary book "The Outliers" proved that any person who has excelled in anything had to practice at least 10,000 hours in that field to reach a level of excellence. People like Bill Gates or the Beatles are such people.

Every new habit you want to establish requires a certain period of discipline. This is the case with dieting, going to the gym or any other undertaking that you might want to take. So, the deeper element of the West involves the ability to create the order of your choosing. This means creating by choice the patterns, structures and relationships you wish to have in your life. This is the work of a lifetime and a most worthy journey.

For you
This ends your personal journey with N.E.W.S.® But in truth, your journey has only begun. The tools and structures of the compass can accompany your personal journey for the rest of your life, if you so choose.
Here is a summary template for you.
Please write inside the compass your main take- away in each direction.

WHERE?
Where are you going?
What is your direction?

___

___

___

HOW?
How do you plan and execute?

WHY?
What motivates you?
What is the meaning of what you do?

WHY NOT?
What are your limiting beliefs and internal barriers?

___

___

___

To go deeper, please visit our website and select a coach to carry on your journey www.newsnavigation.com

PART C - YOUR N.E.W.S.® LEADERSHIP JOURNEY

INTRODUCTION

For you
The next part of this book is dedicated to you, as a current or future leader or manager, or if you wish to become one.

The journey of leadership extends into the four directions of the compass.

It deals with how to lead people, teams and even organizations, according to your scope and your intention.

The world needs a new type of leaders. Former leadership models of the industrial and pre-technological age are no longer relevant. Leadership based on control and fear is a relic of the past that is in the process of disappearing. Leadership is undergoing a major transformation process.

For you
To begin your N.E.W.S.® leadership journey, here are few questions for reflection.

Try to recall an experience you had personally with a great leader.

What was it like? What about that person made you think they were a great leader? What did the leader actually do? Why do you define what they did as leadership?

These questions are very important in order to approach this territory.

There are endless definitions of what leadership is. Here is my current view.

"Leadership is the ability to inspire, direct, engage and move people from where they are to where they can be."

For you
What do you think about this definition?
Does this definition include what you answered about great leaders in your own life and in your journey?
Do you know many leaders like this? Are you such a leader?
Please think about this definition. It has multiple meanings.
Please note that it has to do with helping people move to where they can be, both internally and externally. Let us start our journey this time in the deep end.

For me, the most important thing to say about leadership is that leadership is a conscious choice.

It does not result from nominations or titles.

Management is granted through titles. Leadership is a conscious choice, an ongoing choice, moment by moment.

It governs the way you think, act and respond in various situations. You can lead your family, a group of friends, a team at your place of work, a project, a division and an entire organization.

For you
Is this the choice you have made? If so, let me take you to a journey that starts at the source of leadership.
Leadership from the Inside Out.

Leadership has always been an area filled with mystery, vagueness and speculation.
- Are you born a leader, or do you become one?
- Do leaders respond to needs or situations in the right time and thus become leaders?
- Is leadership based on character or is it based on behavior?

- Can anyone become a leader given the right circumstances?

Few other areas have been as thoroughly researched as leadership, and many theories have been written on the subject.

Some of the theories are based on behaviors. For example, a leader who inspires trust, a leader who conveys vision, a leader who directs different systems, a leader who cultivates and develops talent (S. Covey 2008). The basic idea in this kind of approach is that when one performs these functions with others, they accomplish leadership functions and by doing so, become leaders. Other approaches refer to leadership as a set of behaviors in specific situations i.e Situational Leadership (Blanchard). Additional approaches are based on ethics or character, such as being a servant Leader or a virtuous Leader. These approaches claim that a leader has characteristics such as responsibility, initiative, determination etc. Once a person develops these characteristics, there is a chance that they will become a leader.

I would like to present a somewhat different approach to leadership. This approach is based upon the idea of Leadership from the Inside Out.

The basic idea is that leadership begins by taking inner positions vis-à-vis external reality. These positions often exist in the person before the external need arises.

Once the external need arises the basic internal positions of the person can turn them into a leader.

According to this approach, the basic positions of a person who can become a leader are:

1. I am responsible.
   A person who will become a leader perceives themselves as responsible for the reality around them. They believe that even if they were not responsible for the circumstances, they are responsible for responding and taking care of the consequences. Their responsibility is not theoretical, but practical and immediate. They never point to other people as responsible. They do not blame or complain. They will take a responsible, practical position based on their ability and willingness to influence and solve problems and situations they are confronted with.

Gandhi is a great example of a leader like this.

Living in India, which was divided, split and ruled by the British Empire for hundreds of years, he took the responsibility of solving this situation and freeing India. This commitment led him to persist through a series of complex and sophisticated moves that lasted many years. Gandhi freed the great Indian nation by adopting this position.

2. I create the future reality.
   A person who will become a leader believes wholeheartedly that they can create a desired future reality. They do not focus on current reality, its difficulties and problems. They see current reality simply as a point of departure. Their responsibility is creative. They create a vision from this position. They create a desired future reality and then a path that will lead to this reality. Such a leader considers current reality as the raw material from which they can create a different one – a future reality. If this person is consistent and unwavering with their position, they will motivate others who want the same future reality.

A good example of such a leader is Martin Luther King, who had a vision of a different future reality for black people in the United States. At his starting point this vision seemed impossible to imagine. The reality this generated in the years that followed culminated in the election of Barack Obama for president.

3. I first lead myself.
   A person who will become a leader believes that the onus is on them. Leadership is a movement from existing structures and situations to future structures and situations. Movement necessitates energy and direction. A leader takes the responsibility to lead, and every act of leadership begins with self-leadership. Therefore, a leader is first and foremost focused on leading themselves from undesired structures and realities to desired situations and structures. Out of this self-leadership they establish leadership presence. This presence enables them, over time, to lead others as well towards a desired future reality. Thus, the leader

becomes a personal example and a role model of what they stand for.

Examples of such leaders are: Mother Teresa, who grew up in the slums of Albania and became the leader of a global movement to aid lepers in India.

Jack Welch, who became CEO of GE after starting as an engineer, leading the company to spectacular results.

Lee Iacocca, who grew up as a poor kid in the Bronx and became the leader of Chrysler in its heyday.

Greta Thunburg, a young person, who by setting an example, become the leader of a global movement dedicated to saving the planet.

4. I learn and I develop constantly.
   A person who will become a leader believes that they learn and develop as a way of life. They are open and accept learning, feedback, self-improvement, and development. They do not become too personal or emotionally involved in success or failure but consider them as opportunities for growth. This position increases the trust they get from people around them. It stimulates others to cooperate with them. It enables them to become leaders and to grow and develop throughout their leadership years.

   Thus, they improve over time.

An example of such a leader is Nelson Mandela. As a young man Mandela was incarcerated as a terrorist for the ANC in Apartheid-ruled South Africa. During his years in prison, he studied and developed himself and became an ethical and moral leader who would bring the Apartheid government down non-violently.

There is potential greatness in myself and in others.

A person who will become a leader believes that people have a greatness inside that may not have found its full expression yet. They see it in themselves and are therefore capable of growing, developing and becoming "greater". They also see this potential in others.

A leader believes that people can develop and express more of themselves, more fulfillment, more contribution and more motivation. Part of their leadership involves supporting and enabling people to express their greatness and potential on the path of creating a better reality.

This position also provides the people around the leader with a space to perform, contribute and develop. This becomes attractive to other people. This position is also the basis of charisma - "God's gift" in Greek.

It is said that leaders have charisma - a special divine gift.

In truth, every person comes with an assortment of gifts from birth: different abilities, different skills.

A leader is someone who identifies God's gift within themselves - the talent, the ability and the greatness. This identification enables them to increase the presence of this greatness, work with it, and create with it, until it is recognized by others. These five principles form the inner positions that evolve into leadership capabilities.

Out of these positions a person can face any reality and transform it into a desired future reality. Throughout this process the leader undergoes transformation and translates these internal postures and convictions into actions.

The performance of a leader is derived from these positions. Leaders do not digress from their path despite the challenges they may face along the way.

The way of the leader involves many traps. If the leader falls into these traps, then they will not become a true leader. They will become one of the terrible leaders that the history of the world is littered with. The traps for a leader include:

1. The ego trap - Leadership is not about ego. Leadership is always focused on leading towards a certain vision, a certain potential. It is focused on something that is greater than the leader. A focus on the ego and its importance leads to a pathetic and dangerous kind of leadership. A leadership where the strongest ego dominates all the other ego- driven people. Therefore, we see that great leaders always demonstrate the qualities of simplicity and humility. They consider themselves as a tool or a catalyzing agent that enables the desired reality to materialize and manifest.

   David ben Gurion who led the formation of the new Israeli nation in its homeland is an example of such a humble leader. He led the establishment of the state of Israel and the creation of the Jewish state and was modest

and humble. He lived in a modest wooden hut in the desert.
2. The popularity trap - A leader is not driven by popularity or ratings. Their role is to lead in order to materialize the things they believe in and stand for. Their zeal and inspiration do not require any rating.
3. The image trap – Today, leaders are often preoccupied with projecting an image of leadership but this, too, is a trap. This image consists of clothing, behavior, status symbols, PR and so on and so forth. The leader is surrounded by image consultants who create the desired image they want, according to their opinion and "public opinion." This trap is related to the former two traps. Great leaders do not require an image (Ben Gurion, Gandhi, Mandela), their leadership comes from the inside out, not from the outside in.
4. The zigzag trap - A leader leads to a clear destination. They do not zigzag according to popularity, circumstances or other people's opinions. A zigzagging leader generates mistrust and undermines their own leadership.
5. The power and corruption trap - "Power corrupts. Absolute power corrupts absolutely." This Latin saying is even more relevant today than ever before. Many leaders forget this once they reach senior management or leadership positions. They become intoxicated by power. They often indulge in corruption and lose their vision and sense of mission along the way. They invest all their energy in preserving their status and position and the material benefits that accompany their position (famous examples would be: Idi Amin, Robert Mugabe, Nicolae Ceausescu, Bibi Netanyahu, Bolsonaro, and to some extent Donald Trump and many others).

A leader can avoid these traps by staying alert and aware, focusing extensively on their vision and the situation at large. Such leaders lead businesses, organizations and nations towards a better future.

For you
Do not take this lightly. If after this introduction you are still willing and ready to be a leader, here are some points that will challenge you even further.

Why leadership is even more challenging today?

There are many answers to this question. Here are some for your consideration:

- VUCA world: Volatility Uncertainty Complexity Ambiguity. In a volatile world, people need leadership more than before. They need leaders who can lead despite uncertainty. This is challenging for most leaders as they need to gain people's trust. Nowadays, most people do not have much faith in leaders. So, another important consideration is the ability to build trust.
- Constant changes inside and outside organizations.
  Leading during change is so much more demanding. There is a constant need to be agile, to adapt, to change course whilst staying loyal to a vision or inner calling. The Covid 19 crisis has made this level of change exponentially higher. Leaders need to "read the map" on a weekly basis, as changes are so frequent. Laws, regulations, lock downs, quarantines, and rules all change from one day to the next. Most leaders have never in their lives encountered this amount of change and uncertainty. Most find it extremely challenging and without precedence.
- The need to move fast and together.
  Leadership now needs to be fast, to respond to multiple and frequent changes. You need to move swiftly and guarantee that you keep your people with you. This is very demanding. The current crisis has made it far more complex. With people working from home and teams scattered all over the place, it is most challenging to move together. Yet, the need to move very fast in response to daily changes is paramount.
- The need for alignment.
  When strategies change often as a response to market and economic changes, it is very complicated to stay mobile and aligned to a longer-term, more far-reaching perspective. Most leaders realize now that to keep a team highly aligned, while working remotely, is even more demanding and requires new skills.
- The need for engagement.
  Employee engagement is a global issue. One principal reason for this is the lack of true engaging leadership. There are many operational managers and yet only a handful of real leaders. Most studies show that with the pandemic, engagement of individuals and teams is at an all-time low.

- The need for focus.
  In a context of fast movement, change, information saturation, and overwork, there are many distractions. Leaders must help people set priorities and focus.

For you
Can you see this reality around you?

In this context, a new style of leadership must emerge.

Welcome to the contemporary world of "Participative leadership". This is a new breed of leadership that is emerging in cutting-edge organizations and societies.

The workforce today is very different from the way it was fifty years ago. When most of the world was industrial, most workers did manual labor. The level of expertise needed was quite low, or at least very specific and stable. Workers worked in shifts according to quotas. There were a few senior managers who had higher levels of education, and were responsible for decision-making.

In most modern companies the majority of employees are now what is termed as "Knowledge workers". They are mostly educated. Their main asset is their expertise and their knowledge. They are employed to be creative, innovative, and to solve problems.

Employees like these cannot be managed like workers. They cannot simply be told what to do. They want to understand. They want to influence. They want to take part. If treated like manual laborers, they resist or just leave. This has given rise to participative leadership. The former top-down, industrial way of management is obsolete. The crisis of these times demonstrates this even further. Participative leadership involves people, makes them part of the solution, taps into their resources and intelligence and increases and leverages their buy- in and commitment.

In this context, leadership must involve employees in decision-making to harness their ability and motivation to contribute. This is a radically different leadership paradigm. It requires a complete revamping of the leadership mindset, toolset and skillset. Many "old- school" managers struggle with this shift. It is not simple, and it requires some unique skills. Remote leadership requires even more from leaders.

When the level of uncertainty and ambiguity is almost infinite, people look up to their leaders for answers to fundamental needs. It has always been like that throughout the history of crisis management. Be it war, or natural disaster, people's needs in such times are known and have been recorded over the ages.

In times of crisis, leaders owe their people a clear sense of direction and focus, even when visibility is very poor. This focus or direction can be short-term, with regular updates, allowing for the flexibility required to respond to the constant and rapid changes of times like these.

Leaders need to take into account the human factor much more than before. The human factor goes beyond business and operations. It is the element of leading people as people.

As people are worried and uncertain, leaders need to proactively offer support, encouragement and engagement.

In short, leaders need to discover and develop their own human qualities, beyond their operational excellence, and bring these with them to the workplace. For most leaders this was not necessarily the case before.

So, leaders need to find in themselves those "soft areas" that will enable connection, and therefore a continuation with their teams beyond the crisis.

In times of crisis leaders need to provide transparent and frequent information about what they know and what they do not know, in this way inspiring trust. Employees are not children from whom the grim reality must be hidden. They are adults. With the right information, provided at the right time, they will develop the trust that is so missing in the world at this stage. Leaders can also inspire hope in such times, but it should be open-ended hope, without a deadline. No one knows how long the current situation will last. Therefore, to offer hope with clear deadlines ("by the summer it will be over" etc.) is a mistake. If those deadlines do not come into reality, people will wind up breaking down as morale fades, and psychological resilience is weakened.

Leaders need to be exemplary by choosing to lead themselves first, to reach beyond the boundaries of their own concerns and uncertainties. That is the first thing that is needed. Without self- leadership in times like these, it is very challenging and almost impossible to offer real leadership to others.

Leaders now need to help those that are worried and fearful to overcome their fears, so they can again become fully functional and contributing employees. They need to legitimize people's concerns and not hold these against them. They need to encourage, listen to, and contain peoples' feelings, and offer more optimistic and constructive promoting beliefs. All great leaders like Churchill, Ghandi, and Mandela, to name a few, were able to do this in times of severe crisis.

Lessons from history and from the current crisis suggest that great leaders do all of the things mentioned above.

The issue of real leadership has been neglected for too long. Real leaders lead us from A to B both externally and internally. With the right leaders we grow and develop, while aiming for and reaching new heights of achievements. Not everyone that was nominated as such is fit to be a leader now.

As structures crumble and businesses are heavily disrupted, new types of leaders are needed. They should be able to navigate us even in great uncertainty.

For you
Following, is an introduction for you about the growth and development necessary for all managers and leaders in order to lead in a new and as yet unknown workplace of the 21st century, and within a rolling unprecedented crisis.

There is a growth curve that starts from being an excellent individual contributor in any field. When people are promoted from that position, they usually first become "individual contributor managers", trusting mainly themselves, and turning people into helpers or assistants. This type of first-time manager risks overwork and burnout. Their people do not really develop, since the "superstar manager" does almost everything alone. This continues until the first-time manager realizes that if their team operated more effectively, they could accomplish more with less weight on their shoulders. The growth to high-level operational manager implies leveraging the team's capacity more effectively and efficiently. A well-managed team can produce much more together than any individual alone. Once they realize that the gains are exponential, they start to develop as operational managers. They learn how to set goals, how to track performance, how to use dashboards and scorecards, etc.

Becoming a leader is yet another level all together. A leader is concerned about people. They are concerned about growth. They are concerned about the future. They realize at some point that they can significantly increase the success of their team by making the people in their team more successful. From that moment on, they are focused on making their people more successful.

Genuine leadership comes from a deep desire for achievement to include the drive to see others develop and succeed. This type of leadership is quite rare. This might explain why there is such a trust crisis with leadership in the world today.

For you
If Leadership is still your choice and you are aware of all that is required, here, for me, is the second most important aspect of leadership:

One of my own core concepts is: "At the very heart of leadership lies the ability to navigate".

Navigation deals with leading from the current reality to a desirable future reality, reading the map, understanding the trends, planning and executing the roadmap while engaging people and overcoming obstacles along the way. Navigation involves setting a course and keeping to it. Those who navigate any group of people, team or organization are the actual leaders.

For you
You will now discover how leaders around the world, from micro start-ups to Fortune 100 companies, use the N.E.W.S.® Compass to lead their teams.

When wondering about what a leader actually does, we can use the N.E.W.S.® Navigation Compass to answer this question.

There are five domains of leadership according to the N.E.W.S.® Compass. A leader:

- Knows precisely the current situation of their team at all levels (Reading the Map).
- Provides the Direction and Vision for the future (North).
- Inspires Engagement and Motivation (East).
- Is a Role Model, and Leads their people, and themselves, through Limits and Challenges (South).
- Leads Focused Planning and Execution (West).

Of course, a leader does many other things, but these five definitions will shape the journey you will take in the next chapters.

For you

We invite you now to take your leadership journey with us. This might be motivated by improving the quality of leadership in the world today and as with everything else, it starts with you.

Before setting out on this challenging path clarify for yourself: Who do you intend to lead?

Where to?

Why?

As you answer these questions, please dedicate your leadership journey to the domain revealed by these answers. From here on, I will relate to the people that you wish to lead as "Your Team". They might be at work, in your business, community, group of friends, your family or any other.

Let us explore together the five domains of leadership.

A leader knows precisely the current situation of their team at all levels (Reading the map).

Like any driver who is supposed to know the exact situation and location of their vehicle, so it is with leading your team. You need to know at any given time its location and its situation. Otherwise you cannot really lead them.

When navigating forward as a leader, there are two steps to be taken before setting on your way:
1. Locate the current position of your team.
2. Understand the trends in your environment that will affect your team.

The first thing a GPS does, is locate its current position. This is done by picking up the signal of at least three satellites and locating its place in relation to all three. This is called triangulation – locating your position by three external references. Without knowing where you are starting from, you cannot begin your journey. It is important to note that if you do not know where you are starting with your team, you will all certainly get lost.

The second step is to understand the trends in your environment that might affect your team.

This is a bit like navigating in the sea or in the air. You need to consider the currents or the winds on the way. Otherwise you will aim at getting your team to one location and the currents will take you somewhere else. Over the years I have noticed that many people, teams and organizations navigate their journey without considering their real position and the trends in their environment. This usually results in missing the target altogether. Often these leaders wonder what went wrong, as they had a great strategy and meticulous execution.

When we meet an executive, who is "stuck" or has lost their way, we always explain that "reading the map" is imperative in times of rapid change.

THE FIRST STEP OF YOUR LEADERSHIP PRE-NAVIGATION: ASSESS THE CURRENT POSITION OF YOUR TEAM

The way to assess the current position of your team is through 'triangulation'.

There are many ways and tools with which to analyze the current position. One that we have found very useful is looking at the position of your team in relation to various stakeholders in the environment, as reference points.

These can include shareholders, customers, other teams, other units, managers, employees, vendors, the community, and more.

To understand the position of your team in relation to these stakeholders, you need to assess their needs and then to assess how well you or your team currently respond to those needs. That will reveal to you your team's strengths and weaknesses. The assessment of stakeholders' needs might sometimes be challenging. It might prove useful to actually ask those stakeholders what they need and expect from your team. When the needs of the various stakeholders are clear, the leader or the team can review how well they respond to those needs and where the gaps might be. The appraisal of the current situation must include a multi-faceted perspective: financial, marketing, sales, R&D, employee engagement, management stability, competency, results and more.

When looking at a family or community, other multiple factors factors must be taken into account. This type of information must be frequently available to leaders who navigate their teams or organizations.

The fundamental idea behind this exercise is that "A great team will meet, with excellence, most of the major needs of its most important stakeholders most of the time."

I created this definition more than a decade ago and it is currently more and more accepted by experts and economists. Recently, a group of 180 CEOs of top American companies published a letter where they announced that their companies no longer exist only to maximize profits for shareholders, but rather to meet a much wider set of requirements of other stakeholders. Hallelujah, at last!

This view above is holistic. It is a WIN- WIN equilibrium with all stakeholders and it avoids the classic MBN – Management by Neglect, so common among so many short-sighted leaders. MBN is a situation where all attention and resources are targeted toward one or a few stakeholders while neglecting the rest. This is a short-term approach that is not sustainable.

For you
This definition of a great team takes us to the next exercise. Ask yourself
1. *Who are the major stakeholders for your team?*
2. *What are their most important needs?*
3. *How well does your team currently respond to those needs?*
4. *What do you understand from this overall picture?*
5. *Do all stakeholders get the same "deal" treatment, the same "deal"?*
6. *What is the most acute unanswered need that you need to address when you create the next phase of your team in the North?*

There are of course many other tools to assess the current position of self, team or organization. Some of these tools are financial. Some are comparative studies. Some are benchmarking with other teams around you. Those and many more assessment tools are all relevant. When you are choosing different tools to assess your current position, the more, the better.

Having completed this important overview, it is time to begin to read the map around you.

Aviad Goz

THE SECOND STEP OF YOUR LEADERSHIP PRE-NAVIGATION: READING THE TRENDS IN THE ENVIRONMENT – ORGANIZATION, MARKET, INDUSTRY, OR SOCIETY AT LARGE

This is crucial for the leadership navigation process. Navigating without paying attention to the surrounding currents can lead navigators far away from where they had originally intended to go. This is much like driving a boat in the sea without paying attention to what is happening around you in the water.

Consequently, in real life, an organization's technology might become obsolete; organizational structures might be rendered ineffective, their talents might leave, and their marketing strategy might become irrelevant. Many companies and organizations around the world have experienced this in the past few years. The same applies to teams that do not read the trends inside the organization and do not align themselves accordingly. They may also become irrelevant very quickly. So, early detection of trends, internally and externally, is crucial. Major and minor trends must also be differentiated in order to enhance perspective.

For example, the CEO of a leading global IT company in the 80s said at that time: "There is no reason why anyone would want to have a personal computer in their home. We are not going there". Failing to anticipate consumer/client preferences caused the fall of this major corporation, like so many other giants and many millions of other less known companies.

What is more ridiculous then a personal assistant who still uses a typewriter when applying for a job. Or a programmer in Cobol language trying to join an innovative IT company.

Reading the trends reveals the opportunities and threats that the team or the organization are facing. These can be intrinsic micro-trends or extrinsic, from the macro environment (the marketplace, competitors, regulatory authorities, etc.). Reading trends and anticipating is not simple. It requires a lot of data and the ability to find the needle in the haystack. It requires the ability to connect the dots, and possessing prophetic capabilities. Sometimes it requires luck.

For you
Let us now look at the environment where leadership exists in organizations, communities, or families, and how this changing environment must be taken into account by leaders. Please take into consideration the following changes in trends in the evolving world if you lead a team inside an organization or community.

EARTHQUAKE - THE UNAVOIDABLE TRANSITION FROM ORGANIZATIONS BASED ON SURVIVAL AND CONTROL TO ORGANIZATIONS BASED ON PERSONAL GREATNESS

At this present moment in time, seismic waves are rocking the organizational world. This is an invisible earthquake, taking place on an individual level and when it reaches a magnitude of critical mass, it will erupt, and the full force of its power will be evident. Similar to the breakdown of the communist world, these quakes will have begun well before the collapse. Once it happens, it will be as if it had only taken a few weeks, although the initial waves have been present for years. The global crisis acts as a catalyst for many of these changes. Structures and businesses are currently falling apart.

Since the industrial revolution, thousands of organizations have been established throughout the world with the aim of fulfilling the economic axiom "to maximize profit for owners". In order to maximize profit for one side of the equation, various methods have been developed over time that together have created what will be referred to here as: "an organization based on survival and control". These methods include:

Focus on the bottom line.

The well-known "carrot and stick" method. Endless working hours.

Under-staffing. Rising demands.

Imposition of regular changes.

Threat of redundancy.

Persecution of those who reveal corruption. Organizational politics based on survival.

In this kind of organizational and global environment, the dominating elements are survival and control. They are not talked about or mentioned, yet they are present.

The motto is: "Do as you are told, conform, or you will lose your job, your security and at the very least your chances for promotion".

In this organizational world, some people work fourteen to sixteen hours a day because "this is the norm". They are glued to their cell phones and emails 24/7, because "everyone does it and I am expected to do so as well".

People often do not dare to express their concerns "since it will endanger their standing and their promotion". People suffer from bad managers and incapable leaders in silence, because "they are the boss."

These phenomena are recorded in Kay Gilley's excellent book: "The Alchemy of Fear". Why are people willing to adhere to all those phenomena? The answer can be found in the basic motives of security and stability. Both of these motives were important for the previous generation, the generation of wars, holocaust and survival. These traits were passed on to the next generation as part of its basic education. Beliefs like "learn a profession that will help you make a living", "it's important to find a good job", "there is nothing more important than tenure at work" are not unfamiliar to any of us. It is hard to break the barrier of fears about survival, security and tenure. Many structures are based on those fears, constructed unwittingly by both employers and employees.

It is apparent that in the stable world of organizations and employment, a world based on control and "reward and punishment", there are cracks that are increasing in size.

Firstly, the the psychological contracts of secure employment and vertical mobility have collapsed. Thousands of people have been made redundant, fired, or moved elsewhere through reorganizations, changes, mergers and takeovers.

Secondly, independent, talented workers find themselves trapped in this kind of organization.

After suffering the feeling of being trapped for a number of years, these excellent employees muster up the courage and break out from the organization and become independent, or work as freelancers or subcontractors. Some continue their previous roles and responsibilities as independent freelancers or outsourced resources.

Entire groups of "knowledge-age workers" whose main assets are knowledge, the ability to think, analyze, learn or create are often not willing to respect the orders of poor managers who base their credibility on their hierarchical status. More and more people want to be involved, to have influence, to take responsibility for their future, and most importantly, to fulfill their potential and use their talents. In addition, parents of small children, both men and women, fed up of being allowed to leave work early once a week, are exploring alternative solutions for employment. This is true for "Generation Y" and even more so for "Generation Z" The global crisis has just proved how fast organizations and families can adapt to eminent threat. Working from home would have taken ages to be considered and now it is the new normal. Having the choice of where to work from would have been delayed forever without the current crisis. Let alone the integration of "life" and "work" which was just a remote dream.

During the workshops or lectures I give, I sometimes ask "of all those attending, who fulfills their potential and talent in their present position?" Occasionally one or two hands are raised out of groups of tens or hundreds of people.

Henry Ford had an immortal saying, "When you come to work in my factory, park your brain outside". This is no longer possible in organizations whose success depends largely on the talents and creativity/innovation of their workforce.

These phenomena and others are the cause for a trend where skilled and talented professionals are developing independent employment frameworks, serving organizations as external freelancers. In certain areas of the U.S.A., 30-40% of the workforce are freelance or independent subcontractors, serving the organizations they often used to work for. In some western countries, it is up to 10%, and the trend is increasing.

If this continues, will organizations lose their key talents and depend primarily on outsourcing to excellent, talented individuals? What will happen to organizations who cannot retain talent? The answers to these questions will become clearer in the next few years.

Nevertheless, there are hardly any organizational models that are based on a structure different to the one of survival, control and fear. An alternative model may be an organizational structure based on the greatness and potential of people and not on fear and their basic needs for survival and security. The foundation of such a model is that excellence and personal development become the focus of organizational activity.

It requires a flexible model that allows people to grow, to change positions, to influence and to reach a higher level of contribution. The meaning of this model is not just a scheme or a program for the development of managers, but involves a whole paradigm shift to the Win-Win model, where the aim of the organization becomes creating optimal value for every stakeholder - employees, managers, owners, customers, suppliers, and the community.

This paradigm is a dramatic change in perception of self, organizations, and work itself, as these models develop and companies suffer from more frequent earthquakes. Each seismic change will be accompanied by the loss, from the organization, of its most important talents. There will be increasing frustration in the leadership of organizations when "the carrot and the stick" method will no longer be sufficient. Now as the global crisis persists, more and more people are recalculating their course. More and more people are questioning their career path and feel a deep need to update it.

More and more organizations of the future, driven also by personal development and excellence, are emerging. These are usually small organizations, or autonomous divisions inside larger organizations, usually growing around future-oriented leadership.

For you

Will you be part of such future leadership? Is this something you are willing to go for?

To finalize the reading of the map in order to navigate forward, here are some final questions to consider:

What are the recent trends in your industry or environment?

Will there be a need for what you and your team do 10 years from now? Where is technology going to in your field of expertise?

What does it all say? What needs to be done? what needs to be changed or be realigned? When you know your current position and you can read the map of important and impactful trends around you, you are ready to embark on your dynamic leadership navigation journey.

YOUR LEADERSHIP JOURNEY IN THE NORTH

North Leadership mindset "It is my responsibility with my team to set our direction, strategy and vision."

For you
Let's begin your North Leadership journey with a rather exceptional, true story.

The story of Selina
Selina is a haven for nomads, travelers and explorers.
"Selina is not just accommodation. Yes, we offer (gorgeous, beautifully designed) accommodations. More than that, we offer a place to connect with others and be inspired by stunning beaches and lush jungles. Fuel your creativity in energetic urban centers. Catch a wave, dance until dawn, or tap into a new level of productivity with surfing, activities, co-working, and community by Selina. If you're looking for a unique, immersive, purpose-filled experience, you're looking for Selina."
From: www.selina.com

I met Rafi and Daniel in 2011. They were young real estate entrepreneurs in Panama. They developed neighborhoods on land they acquired near the Pacific coast. In an Organizational Navigation process that I ran with them for their real estate company, their direction of Greatness was created. It was to focus on developing assets that are close to the beach and can create special added value. This was in 2013. One of the assets that they bought was a small hotel in a fishing village, called Pedasi in the Azuero peninsula in Panama. These phenomena and others are the cause for a trend where skilled and talented professionals are developing. As they operated this hotel, they took note of the kind of guests that were arriving and what their needs were. They realized that many of their guests were travelers that wanted to travel the world, visit "cool" places, while working remotely and staying connected. This type of traveler is now called "Digital Nomad".

Apparently, there are an estimated 200 million young people who prefer to live this unique lifestyle. They examined this more in depth and realized that there is a global movement of growing numbers of young millennials making the choice to travel and work from a distance. Then they had an incredible vision: They would create a network of specialized hostels for this kind of traveler throughout Central and Latin America. The network would cater to their specific, unique needs. They would have at least 40 locations in the region, and they would call the concept "Selina". The headquarters would be in Panama City.

This vision was quite bold, for they had neither the necessary resources or even the know-how of the hospitality industry. Yet, this vision was within their direction of Greatness. It inspired them, and they went for it with total conviction, commitment and dedication. It takes courage and belief to go for this kind of vision. They started the first Selina location in Playa Venao, a surfing beach near Pedasi. The place was designed in a totally new way and included surfing, experience, parties and a co- working space. The success was tremendous. The place was over-booked and many flocked to spend time with the surfers in this amazingly beautiful location. They went on to envision a new concept in hospitality: Amazing locations with activities, experiential content, great teams of young people, co-working spaces and a place that would go beyond the concept of hotels and hostels and offer opportunities to share experiences and meet people.

The concept of hosting young digital nomads went viral. They expanded to a few more locations in Panama. Then they extended to the whole region of Central America – Costa Rica, Guatemala, Honduras, Nicaragua. Then into South America, Colombia, Peru, Ecuador, Argentina, Brazil and more. Two years later, they had 1,500 employees in a bubbling, dynamic, beautifully chaotic fast-growing company.

With fast growth came many challenges of management, organizational development, development of managers, establishing processes and structures. At this stage we were asked to run N.E.W.S.® Organizational Navigation for Selina. This process occurred two years in a row.

The first one took place in El Valle in Panama and the second was in London and New York. We were contracted to help in setting goals and finally in creating the leadership academy for Selina. We accepted the challenge gladly. At this stage Selina attracted attention as a disruptive power in the global hospitality industry arena.

In the following year, Selina expanded to the US and Europe. Its headquarters moved to London and New York to cater to multinational activity. They started urban locations in San Jose, Medellin, Porto, Miami and New York. With all that expansion, the concept of Selina was refined and became more and more clear. In four short years, Rafi and Daniel found themselves leading a global giant, valued at more than one billion dollars. Selina now has over 85 locations. They design their locations using recycled materials. They work with local artists and artisans everywhere they go. They integrate the local community and contribute back to it with the "Selina gives back" program. They create hydroponic greenhouses to grow the vegetables for their guests. They serve healthy foods and have created a culture of wellness. The list of activities in Selina playgrounds includes yoga classes, cooking lessons, dance, surf, adventure stories, local tours, local art, connecting with people, sharing and more.

Was this an easy journey? No way. It was full of leadership struggles, gaps, missing processes and lack of critical personnel. There was a need to raise funds, to develop managers, to separate from some people and to welcome others into the teams.

The Selina team is a courageous group of people daring to do the impossible. Every visionary journey looks like this in its own way. If not, it is probably not a new and disruptive vision.

We work with a handful of companies like Selina with great vision and fast growth, and they are absolutely inspiring. Selina has since updated its vision. Now it aims to have 400 locations worldwide, including in Europe, the US, and Asia. Their journey continues, and we are very happy to be part of it. Even with the crisis bringing most tourism around the world to a halt, Selina prevails.

They transformed many of their hostels into more permanent residences for this time. Against all odds, they raised investments and continued opening new locations. Rafi and Daniel have grown into leaders of a multinational fast-growing giant, with more growth and expansion on the horizon.

For you
The role of a leader in the North is very unique.

What leaders do in the North is the very essence of leadership. They give their people a clear sense of the future. They foster hope and confidence in the ability to reach that future. They engage their people deeply with the drive to grow, to make a difference. I would like to equip you with some best in-class tools and frameworks. for leading teams in the North. It could be any team with any mission – family, society, volunteering, organizational, business, community, and any other.

INTRODUCTION TO YOUR LEADERSHIP JOURNEY IN THE NORTH

When the joint direction for the future is clear to everyone in the team or organization, everyone follows the same direction. This makes it possible to achieve a high level of execution.

Getting 100% alignment in a team is ideal. It secures long-term execution, loyal clients, and involved and committed employees.

This is an ideal situation. It is quite rare to find this in reality. What we usually face is the more typical situation where individuals have their own opinions or priorities and are not connected to the team direction and goals. It is possible that these team members:

Don't know the strategic goals.

Don't know how to achieve them.

Don't know what they personally are supposed to do to help the organization achieve the goals.

Don't share responsibility for execution.

The result of this typical situation is slow movement, weaker execution, procrastination, and weak performance.

The worst scenario is when team members have individual priorities and are not connected to the team direction and goals. In such cases, the team's vision cannot be achieved and chaos ensues. Such teams sometimes have to be dismantled altogether because of their poor performance.

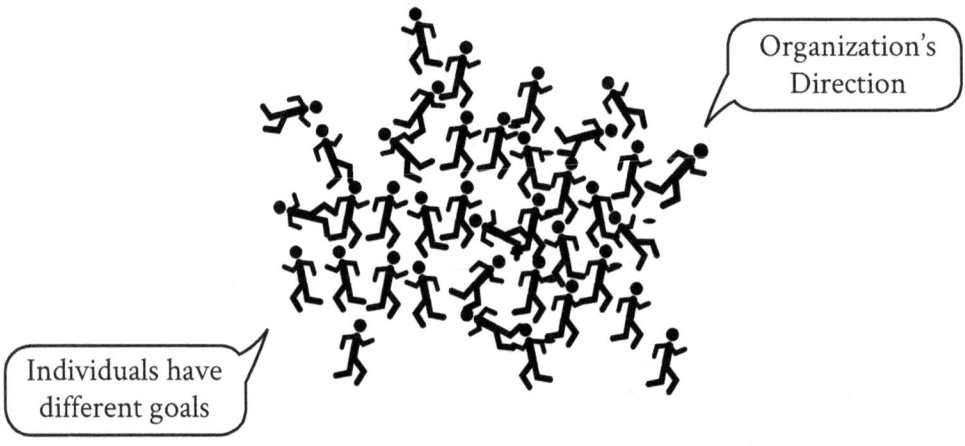

For you
What is the level of alignment of the team that you lead? How did it come about?

Creating the next chapter for your team will be very similar to the individual journey in the North. However, it requires different practicality and different skills.

Teams can follow a North strategic line that has three stages:
1. Define their direction of greatness and the next step.
2. Define strategic drivers.
3. Create together your practical vision.

Visually the Leadership journey in the North will look like this:

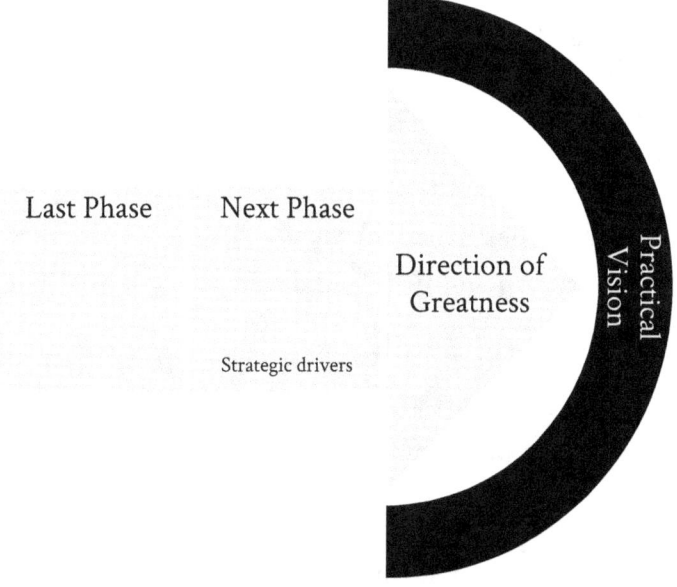

These are top tools and best practices applied with thousands of teams across the globe.

Let us take an example: You might lead a team of friends that want to make your neighborhood more environmentally friendly. You have worked out your direction of Greatness:

"To build new and better lifestyle for the neighborhood community." You have decided that the next phase of your journey as a team is:

"To get started". This is an initial phase that will require few areas of focus. The strategic drivers or areas of focus that you have agreed upon are:

1. Locate community members who want to volunteer, and work with them regularly.
2. Lead a major cleaning process in the neglected areas of the neighborhood.
3. Involve the children of the neighborhood in planting small gardens in designated areas.
4. Apply for assistance from the municipality.

You agreed that your practical vision is: That in two years the neighborhood will be clean. There will be 5-6 small gardens. The gardens will also have fruit trees for the community to enjoy. At least one of the gardens will have a little playground for children, and the municipality will help and contribute. One garden will be for elderly people to meet and will include facilities for their dogs.

Let us take a very different example: This is an HR team in an organization. They worked out that their direction of Greatness is: "To develop people and talent in the organization."

They agreed that the next phase for them will be:

"Launch programs for identifying and developing talents." They decided their strategic drivers are:
1. Creating onboarding process for all new employees.
2. Building process to identify talents.
3. Designing training programs for all new employees and particularly for identified talents.
4. Setting up coaching and mentoring processes throughout the organization, focused on talent development.

Their practical vision is that in 3 years' time, the organization will achieve a retention of 90% of the identified and developed talents, who will advance to responsible positions in the organization.

A new D.N.A. of management and leadership style will be developed. Everyone in the organization will graduate from a training or coaching process that will prepare them to address the employment needs of the next decade; and finally, that the employee satisfaction score will increase by at least 20%. Finally, Consequently, there will be a better atmosphere and vibe throughout the organization.

For you

Do you have such a future strategic focus worked out with your team?

If you want to lead your team to such a North, you need to know that it will require from you three things:

Create   Engage   Manage

You will need first to create your team's North in your own mind.

Then you need to engage the team and ensure buy-in (remember participative leadership?) Finally, you will have to manage it from day to day, from week to week, until it is achieved.

THE CREATE PHASE - CREATE THE NEXT CHAPTER OF YOUR TEAM ON THE DIRECTION OF ITS GREATNESS

If we liken the development of any team to a story, we will find that teams have different chapters in their evolution.

A chapter can be short or long and is characterized by major changes.

The first step in creating a new North for a team is always to look at the previous chapter and understand what it was all about. You always want to look back before moving forward. You need to ask yourself a few questions about the last phase of your team:

What has our main focus been recently?

What name can we give to what actually happened?

Giving a name is a powerful tool to capture the deep essence of what has occurred.

Here are some names that teams and organizations have chosen, by way of example: "The birth of a gorilla", "Reaching base camp one", "Total chaos", "A time to stop being victims", "Changing generations".

For you
Choose a name for the last phase of your team or organization, since the last changes you can recall.

After choosing a name, you need to answer the following questions:

As we move forward from the last phase, what changes are needed now? Minor changes?

Major changes?

No change at all?

Or a complete transformation to the "next version" of the team?

Almost all teams go through similar "life cycles". This can be likened to the growth of a tree.

This idea of life cycles of teams and organizations was brought forward by Itzhak Adizes who describes the growth and change of organizations using nature as an analogy.

Every organization or team starts as an idea – "a seed". This is a very innovative stage.

If the seed develops and manifests in practical terms, the team is born, much like a plant shooting its first green leaves above ground. Then, if all goes well, it grows fast and becomes a "start-up" very fast, disorganized, and hectic moving forward. This is much like the thin stem of a tree, growing fast but still fragile. Then the tree needs to thicken. Likewise, the organization or the team need to begin to build processes, structures, management routines, so that it will not break down or disperse. Then comes maturity, where the team or the organization gets organized, stabilizes and is properly managed. Much like a mature balanced tree.

This of course is a best-case scenario, given that teams and organizations may not transition smoothly from one stage to the next. The decline of organizations and teams also follows a "classic" cycle. Innovation is the first element to disappear. Practicality and growth are second. The processes and functioning structures are the third to go, and so on.

As teams and organizations go through their cycle of life, their needs change and evolve. At first, they need innovation. Then they need practicality. Then they need processes and interface work etc. When they go to a new market, they need new people, talents, localization and more. Then they need stability and on-going sustainable growth and consolidation.

Very often when exploring the next phase for a team or organization, the answer lies within the transition between those life cycles and the needs they bring about. This is a classic approach and yet in the changing world today, cycles happen faster, and sometimes simultaneously, and in different directions.

It is imperative that the team's next phase be created together with team members.

According to Jim Collins, author of "Good to Great", great teams and organizations make choices based on the "Greatness Model".

We have used the model for the personal journey in the North. Originally it was created for organizations and it has been validated over the years.

Teams and organizations that choose their direction by asking these three important questions eventually become highly motivated teams and achieve great results.

The order of the questions in this model is very significant.

1
What are we passionate about as an organization?

2
What are our core competencies and capabilities?

3
How can we meet the needs of our market in a practical manner?

(Adapted from Jim Collins)

This model is designed from the inside out. Teams must find a direction that aligns with the answers to these three questions.

Those teams can then follow their uniqueness and make a substantial contribution to their organization. The same applies to the entire organization and its unique contribution in the marketplace.

Developing a direction and following this model creates great results. It is much like in the old story of the "Fox and the Hedgehog". The fox knows many things but is disabled by his opportunistic, ever-changing approach. The hedgehog, on the other hand, only has one "big" idea and focuses on that. The hedgehog always wins. In the rapidly changing world, it is imperative to be flexible and agile. However, at the same time there is a need for some constants - consistency and stability. The constants can be created by adhering firmly to the direction of Greatness and not deviating from it. By analogy this is like having a backbone. This backbone allows for the agility or flexibility. Without this kind of backbone, the team or the organization could become dispersed and chaotic.

The "Good to Great" companies follow the "hedgehog" approach and focus on their inner circle of uniqueness. The origin of a team's authentic direction is to be found where these three circles intersect: What you are passionate about as a team needs to meet the team members strong talents, core capabilities, and competencies. These two are constant. They need to meet the organizational and market's current needs. This is the variable that keeps changing all the time. Therefore, the meeting point moves all the time. It is the role of leadership to identify this moving meeting point and strive towards it.

The same process can be conducted with senior leadership teams to navigate the whole organization, externally and internally.

Here are some examples of the Direction of Greatness that were discovered by a number of organizations that we work with:

"To lead big data analytics to prevent crime and fraud".

"To develop the purest distillations of medicinal plants for Chinese medicine practitioners".

"To develop the students' market by supreme self- learning programs".

"To make our customers successful by optimizing their billing systems".

"To support artists in developing their international careers".

If these sounds a bit like "mission statements", this is not a coincidence. When connecting the inner passion and capabilities of a senior management team to the needs of the market and their various stakeholders, that is what is created. Most "Mission statements are fancy 'wannabe' statements created without an "inside – out" approach. The process of finding authentic direction from the inside out using the Greatness model is much more powerful and real.

The next phase should always be within the boundaries of the "Direction of Greatness" because this is where the organization or the team want to go. It is very easy to get tempted by various business opportunities, as many of my clients do. Then to find your team after a while far away from what people love to do and are good at. Eventually this results in lack of engagement and motivation, burnout and loss of identity. The 'Greatness' approach, however, fosters the organic growth of teams and organizations. They grow in the domain where they provide a unique added value and contribution, and eventually experience success.

For you
What is the Direction of Greatness of your team? What is the next phase for your team?

Please give this exercise some time and consideration.

Now let's make this even more practical.

CREATE YOUR TEAM'S PRACTICAL STRATEGY

At this point, it is now time to define the practical strategy that will drive this next phase. To lead your team in the North, you need to provide them with the practical strategy that can lead them forward. One of the simple strategic tools for a team are the strategic drivers. Strategic drivers are the main areas of focus, the main projects and the main initiatives. Strategic drivers need to be both practical and high level. Most importantly, there should be very few, only 3-5 in all. This is important because it allows the team or the organization to focus and not get dispersed. Very often teams and organizations wish to move forward on too many projects and areas of focus. Most studies show that having more than 3-5 areas of focus at a given time leads to dispersion. It is often not easy to choose. Therefore, a lot of teams are not really focused and disperse their energies across a wide range of topics. Eventually instead of doing much they end up doing very little. Focus is the name of the game.

Working with many executive teams on the challenge of refining the strategic drivers inspired me to create a solution that will assist people and teams to focus. So, I created the Six S mode™. Working with this model allows smooth transitions from the previous phase to the next one. Some strategic drivers need to keep on going. Some need to start. Some need to change. Here is the full model of moving from one phase to the next.

The 6S Model
What should we stop doing? STOP!

What should we do less of? SLOWDOWN!

What should we do more of? SPEED UP!!

What should we start doing? START!

What should be carried on but differently? SAME BUT DIFFERENT!

What should be carried on? SAME!

To choose their strategic drivers for the next phase the team needs to decide what they should...

Stop altogether

Slow down (do less of).

Speed up (do more of).

Start anew.

Continue, but differently.

Continue from the previous phase with no changes.

These guidelines will support the team in defining the new strategic drivers. The process of choosing strategic drivers needs to be done in agreement and consensus. Usually a skilled facilitator can help a great deal in achieving this.

For you
To attempt to lead such a participative discussion is not easy. Let me introduce a special tool set that I developed and which is called FPPC.

The FPPC are abbreviations of: Frame, Pull-Push, Conclude.

This is a tool set to create participation and engagement.

Frame – Give the topic background and context, the reason for the discussion and its aims.

Pull – Ask a few well-prepared questions so that participants express their views in the matter.

Push – Add your view and ideas.

Conclude – summarize the various viewpoints and lead to conclusion.

To conduct a discussion like this requires that you come prepared with your ideas, so you know what you want and yet stay open to the different views of your team. Most managers have to be trained to lead such discussions. When you lead discussions in this way you implement the idea of – Engage.

For you

So, first you Create your views and ideas as a leader and then you Engage the team by leading a participative discussion.

Can you do this?

Are you willing to try?

This is probably one of the best ways to stimulate and ensure team engagement and buy-in.

Because they create with you, they share ownership. Nothing can replace that sense of ownership.

So, now you are ready to engage your team and create together your strategic drivers for the next phase.

Examples of strategic drivers from various teams and organizations I worked with:

"To develop our consultants as lead generators".

"To implement the new ERP system across the board".

"To improve internal communication and get everyone on board with the new strategy and vision".

"To disrupt the market by offering our low-cost solutions". "To create the next level management".

"To create a new specialized solution for accountants". "To finally go to market".

"To develop our SME business and scale it".

As you can see, these strategic drivers relate to all kinds of both internal and external needs of the team or the organization.

CREATE AND ENGAGE YOUR TEAM WITH A PRACTICAL VISION

Now, we approach together what is probably the most known and effective leadership tool – practical vision.

The concept of "Vision" has many interpretations. For some it relates to some overall aspiration. For others it is a dream or an illusion. For me, as stated earlier, "vision" has its original meaning – the ability to see a picture in the future.

Research shows that imagining events such as winning, achieving your goal, or reaching the summit of a mountain has an exhilarating effect. It can release the same neuro- peptides in the brain and the body as the actual event. The greater the imagination and immersion in the vision, the more energy and positive chemistry your team will enjoy! Your aim is to create a joint vision with your team. Have you ever done it before? Have you involved your team actively in creating the joint vision? If not, now is a good time to begin.

When a group of people envisions the future together in the same way, a great creative power is released. When the intentions of many are aligned, they create a vector that can shape the future reality and the way of things to come.

Imagination is the main faculty that people need in order to create a vision. People have the power to create their future reality. They can visualize the best-case scenario for themselves in the future. If a team follows their direction, employing their strategic drivers, what will their reality look like? What will the best-case scenario be, in two or three years?

This kind of Vision is like a lighthouse. It gives people hope and the energy to achieve great achievements.

Everything in the human world was once in someone's imagination.

Everything, from the clothes we wear, to the buildings we live in, all the way to the companies we work for.

All were once in the imagination of a person or a group of people.

The question then arises: Why do most people/teams not have such a vision? The reasons are many. Most of them originate from the N.E.W.S.® South.

1. Fear of failure. Most people do not attempt much, for the bolder the ambition, the greater the probability of failure. If people do not intend anything daring, there is no danger that they might fail.
2. Fear of committing to their vision. It is more comfortable to go with the flow. Commitment requires discipline, moving out of the comfort zone and other uncomfortable practices.
3. People do not believe they can create a vision and live up to it. This usually comes from lack of knowledge or understanding about the usefulness of such a tool as a vision.
4. Educational system oriented to practicality, results and logical thinking, instead of developing people's imagination and creativity.
5. Unrelenting pressure from boards for short-term results rather than long-term vision and impact.

An effective vision that can shape the future must have a few characteristics.

It needs to be specific and not general, because only by being specific can you create.

It needs to be tangible, positive, daring and attainable. Experience with practical visions shows that these specifications increase the probability of the vision to actually occur. The practical vision does not need to be realistic at the current point in time. Otherwise why would we need imagination?

For you
To help you create a practical vision with your team, here are some great highly effective tools that we use with hundreds of teams and organizations every year.

The first tool is more suited for rational and logical teams. Together write a report of a successful year three years into the future. This report should take into account the successful implementation of the strategic drivers over the next few years.

The second option is more for creative innovative teams. This approach involves creating reality with all its different aspects.

The team may imagine an article published in their organizational newsletter or in a leading trade publication in their particular field or market 3 years from now.

In this article, they need to describe their achievements and successes over the past year, their specific contribution to the team or organization or to the market, and the reaction of each stakeholder. Ask them to imagine and aim high.

The third great tool is to envision a future event of the team or the organization, where different speakers will summarize a successful year in a few years' time. The frame is: "If we go in our direction of Greatness and follow our strategic drivers, what will success look like?"

These tools are highly effective as they bypass usual forms of imagination and invite people to imagine in practical framework. When a group creates this kind of shared picture in the future it aligns them and creates a very strong vector of progression.

For you
Try to envision, your team, your organization or your business three years from now.

If the next three years are to be successful, what will your main achievements be? What will your financial situation be?

How will your internal or external clients respond? What kind of projects will your team be involved in?

What will the team spirit and culture be like?

Try to envision this future picture as tangibly and as vividly as you can. Do these tools actually work?

A number of companies that I have worked with, for some consecutive years, wondered about the validity of this tool. The CEOs of these companies checked the joint vision that we had created three years earlier for their organizations. We were all amazed! The actual results three years after creating the vision as part of the first Organizational Navigation™ process were very similar to the practical vision. Even the financial elements of revenues, valuation and profits showed accuracy of 10% above or below the numbers in the vision, despite the fact that the practical vision those teams set was very bold, bordering on the impossible!

It is important to mention that these imagination and envisioning exercises were not done based on a linear progression forecast. Thus, the amazing power of collective imagination to shape the future.

For you
Your leadership journey in the North ends here. It should be repeated each year and sometimes each quarter, as reality changes and organizations continue to grow and develop. In uncertain times of global crisis, the need to set a clear North despite poor visibility becomes even more necessary. Actually. it needs to happen much more often. Some companies I work with now do this exercise every quarter or even every six weeks, while reading the map of opportunities and threats that changes very quickly.

The following chapter is dedicated to the significance of having mutual intentions in a group of people, in this case, an organization.

WHERE IS MY ORGANIZATION GOING?

Think about the last time you took a flight or went on a bus or a train journey. The most important thing you wanted to know was the destination of the journey. It is easy to assume that, although the adventure could be fun, you and most people would not board a vehicle with an unknown destination.

Now think about the organization you work for or belong to. Do you know where it is going? Do you know its destination clearly? You might say "my organization tries to maximize profits for shareholders or owners. This is where it is going", but this is very generic and does not really specify any clear direction or destination.

Millions of people go to work every day in companies and organizations around the globe without the slightest idea where their organization is heading. You can adapt to it. People can become accustomed to almost anything, even if it is strange and bizarre.

Let's examine what happens to a person who works in an organization and yet does not have a clue about where it is going, or in other words, does not know the direction, strategy or future vision of those who lead the organization. First of all, the person will find it difficult to identify and set priorities, which are derived from the big picture. In the absence of a broader perspective, priorities will be determined according to convenience, stress, personal preferences and other biases. Eventually the person will be sucked into daily, mundane and routine activities that are not aligned to any larger, more collective contribution. You might say, "But people might have personal objectives that their managers defined for them and the managers have their own objectives and goals that someone up the ladder defined for them and probably that someone knows the direction and the overall picture". That might be so, but this view is a heritage of the industrial age where a select few at the top were supposed to think for the many who were supposed to do only routine manual work. This hardly applies today. Many people in organizations are "knowledge-age workers". They are educated, often experts in their fields. They are required to think, analyze, and create solutions. They cannot really be operated by telling them "Here is your objective. Do it. You do not need to understand more than simply the task at hand. Just sit in the bus and do your thing. The driver will take you somewhere and it is none of your business where".

Secondly, the level of engagement and internal motivation of people lacking direction and a vision of the larger picture will be quite minimal. People have a very basic need to be part of something bigger, to contribute to a larger cause. If the organization does not provide this opportunity, people will seek ways to express their true motivation and calling through hobbies, social media, or other activities. They will need to be externally motivated through increasing compensation, rewards or various other carrot-like incentives. Work will become a means and not an end. "This boring meaningless work allows me at least to go on weekends to my mountain cabin where I really have a great time and do what I really love". Again, this may seem normal or common, but if you look at it from an external point of view, you might agree that it is strange to spend most of your time doing something you are not connected to, so that for a small part of your time you can do what really matters to you. People who are not engaged at work, cause much damage to themselves and to others around them and this attitude is contagious.

Thirdly, when you do not know the direction or purpose of your organization, you are bound to make mistakes even if you mean well. In the military, a commander always needs to know the larger picture of the battlefield beyond their own specific tactical assignments. Knowing the larger picture prevents fatal mistakes. Millions of dollars are wasted in organizations because of unsynchronized, unaligned initiatives and efforts. This can happen due to over-inflated egos of managers but will surely happen when there is no alignment to a clear direction and strategy. I have encountered so many situations where unaligned initiatives of various individuals or teams in organizations were canceled later or totally changed. This creates chaos, waste of resources and eventually a lack of consistency and trust. Trust comes into the picture because internal consistency in the midst of changing external circumstances builds trust in organizations and their leaders. Unfortunately, consistency is ignored by many leaders of organizations. Most people will then refrain from engaging in their work so that their "cogwheels" are not broken due to lack of consistent direction and far too frequent changes.

Lack of cooperation is the last factor that will result when people do not know where the organization is going. People will tend to focus on personal goals or interests or in the best case, on their unit's goals and interests. This creates separation and protection. Units or teams stop cooperating. Managers protect their teams from the "overall chaos". Many managers in organizations actually use those words.

If there is no one comprehensive and over-arching target and initiative, people and units will create their own. The problem is that these smaller arrows will point in different directions making cooperation and alignment virtually impossible. The combined impact, power and speed of all these small non-aligned arrows is very small compared to what could happen if all the arrows are aligned and to create one combined, integrated effective large arrow. The reality that I meet daily in companies where people do not know where the organization is going is that each person or team guards their interests, communication is lacking, cooperation is missing, and people are overly busy with trivial non-productive activities. The organization feels chaotic and organizational progression is very slow if at all.

So, why don't leaders communicate the overall direction, strategy and vision effectively to all people in their organizations? Why in many cases do they not share where the organization is going?

I think sometimes it is because they themselves do not know or are not very clear. I have seen many small and large organizations moving forward with some kind of inertia, often finding it difficult to agree where the whole thing is going. Sometimes they might have a vague idea, not well defined or outdated, or simply a set of blurred ideas. Obviously, this would be hard to communicate. Or the leadership team is split in its views and cannot reach a consensus. This can happen due to different interests, interpersonal battles or points of view. Each senior manager then orients their unit in a different direction, resulting in conflict and lack of cooperation and coordination.

There are some situations where the leadership clearly defines where the organization is going. They do serious strategic processes but then do not inform others in the organization. Or once a year they send out an e-mail message with very general ideas that are soon forgotten. Such as "We will lead the market… blah, blah, blah…"

Why? Often senior management believes that only they should know information involving direction and strategy. That it is almost a secret which should be hidden from competitors and even from their own employees. They often believe that they should translate the direction and strategy for others into segmented units or personal objectives and keep the larger picture to themselves.

I believe these tendencies, however sincere, simply belong to another era where the wise were at the top and the less intelligent, educated or skilled, below. I believe leadership owes it to its people. People need to understand where the organization is going. They need to be involved in the larger picture. A yearly message or a brief corporate meeting is not enough. The direction and strategy should be discussed on many levels in the organization. People need to understand their part in it. How can they contribute? How does it impact or determine priorities? What does it mean to their roles in practical terms?

This is a process that leadership teams can lead. The rewards for organizations that actually do this kind of process are many. People actually understand. They find it easier to commit. Many become more engaged and motivated. Very often cooperation and productivity grow, and results improve.

This is not just a nice HR idea. It has been proven by serious studies that this kind of approach and these practices actually improve organizational results and create better cultures in organizations. Is it easy? No.

Do you need to get out of the industrial management mindset? Yes. Is it possible? Yes.

I must admit that I personally started my leadership journey as a team leader in a pharmaceutical company. I was 25 years old at the time. I was vain. I thought I knew it all. I commanded everyone around. I kept my overall views to myself. I was a solo player with a few assistants around, which I called a team. I created a team that was not great, although it had great people in it, some of whom became CEOs in later years. I had to learn and unlearn so much to know what I know today about leadership and management.

This is therefore based on the hope that things can be different for all.

For you
Welcome to the East leadership journey of meaning, motivation and inspiration.

YOUR LEADERSHIP JOURNEY IN THE EAST

Leadership state of mind "It is my job to inspire and engage my team".

For you
Let me invite you to the real story of a huge company I was working with and their journey in the East.

The Story of one of the "Big Four"
"Our purpose is to build trust in society and solve important problems."

This is part of the mission statement of a large global company that I had the opportunity to work with.

This company is one of the four largest companies in their field globally. It exists in every country where it operates in partnership. The partnership employs hundreds of thousands of people globally. It is a very large company, but yet it is run as a partnership. I worked with them in one of their largest subsidiaries. The initial request was from the leadership of that partnership to help them with their culture. They wanted to create a more collaborative culture, a culture of true partnership based on deep, real discussions. They said that most of the interactions between them were very business-oriented and the whole spirit of partnership was not enough at play. Their own internal surveys were showing that partners did not feel sufficiently engaged and wanted a shift in the cultural emphasis from being mainly business oriented to being partnership oriented, as well. "We want to discuss what this partnership actually means. What is the reason for our existence? "We want to go really deep in those discussions" said the Chairman with whom I conversed a few times. This sounded to me like a deep East direction. The questions "Why do we exist? What is important in our partnership?"

are the questions to explore in the East. The online assessment that we sent to the participants showed a very wide range of views amongst the 40 partners that we were going to meet. There was no common view of what this partnership was, what was important about this partnership, and even where it was heading.

We met the 40 partners in an exotic remote location. All very serious people with many years' experience in their fields. Some of them had been with the firm for over forty years and some were younger "stars", partners who had joined recently.

As we started, it became clear that there was a significant difference between the old school of partners who have been around for many years and the young "stars" who had quite different views about what partnership is and what is important about it. The older members were very much for values like shared responsibility, mutual support, backing each other and the like. The new younger members were much more business-oriented and individualistic in their approach. It became clear that this organizational navigation was going to be challenging. Moreover, I was told that there were 400 other partners and that whatever process we did with the first 40 partners, we would have to also do with the rest. The mammoth task was to create one agreed culture, a single agreed reason for existence, shared values amongst 40 partners and then among 400 partners. This was not easy. It was probably one of the most challenging organizational navigations that I had ever conducted. The process was intense. The very logical participants became quite emotional.

We started our journey in the East, which is unusual. In the process the participants realized that although their views were different, there were areas of similarity. I used a Venn diagram to show them the different areas, but also the areas that overlapped in their different views. We focused the discussion on the overlapping areas (I was always a peace maker). We managed to catalyze some agreements about what was important for all of them. We then moved to the North and discussed how to navigate the partnership forward, not the organization but the partnership. They crafted strategic drivers and nominated champions and teams for each strategic driver for the partnership to become real. They came up with a practical vision of best-case scenario for the partnership. People became more and more open and enthusiastic. We looked at their South and what might stop them. Their common limiting belief was: "Tomorrow we go back to a metrics-driven business environment and all this nice stuff will disappear".

We worked it out and broke through that belief. Finally, we created a plan in the West for how to go about it throughout the year and keep it going to reach critical goals. A week later, I spoke with the Chairman. He was more excited than I had ever heard him before. "It was amazing" he said "I did not believe we would get to such agreements. Everyone is full of energy to go and do what we have decided". Then he was back to his reasonable, careful self and he said, "Let us see if they come back with plans in three months as they all committed to do". Then he called and said "plans submitted as promised. Let us now bring the 400 other partners to the same state as the first 40. This is going to work….". I met the other 400 partners in large groups with the intent of creating the miracle again on a larger scale. The meetings took place in three major cities. More than a hundred people attended each of them. The first 40 partners brought forward their ideas form the first session of how to create the next phase of partnership. Then we moved into discussions. The discussions were intense. Many of them were very strong- minded experts. There were points where I wasn't sure it would end well. But I trusted the process. And almost miraculously we ended the discussions in each city with overwhelming agreements of the participants. Moreover, upon my request we had 150 partners volunteer to be active "Change Agents "to bring about the next phase in their journey as a partnership. A year later, in the middle of the Covid 19 crisis I learned that these "change agents" are still active and that the plans are being well executed.

YOUR LEADERSHIP JOURNEY IN THE EAST - INTRODUCTION

"Culture eats strategy for breakfast." Peter Drucker

Cultures are formed around codes. This is a bit like crystals inside saturated solutions that define the way of crystallization. Cultures can be created without consciousness or awareness, just by implicitly accepted patterns of behavior. Cultures can also be created with great care and attention. The codes around which cultures form are sometimes called values. Every group of people living or working creates a culture.

Sometimes, there is a need to examine the values of a team and translate them into what they actually mean.

The work in the East is about creating a team culture. In larger organizations it will be a team culture in line with the organizational culture. In independent teams it will be the work of the leader to define with the team the codes and values they want to foster in mutual cooperation. The issue of common culture is often disregarded as an important issue. However, the rise and fall of empires, nations, organizations and teams rely greatly on their mutual culture and its strength.

Functional teams work to identify the existing de facto values that allow them to succeed. This is a process of discovery.

New, or non-functional teams work to define desired values or "wannabe" values that are missing and need to be developed for the team to progress. This is a process of joint creativity.

Exploring and creating values together creates a code for common behaviors, clear expectations, and shared meaning. Many are mistaken in believing that a leader can set the values for their team by themselves. If people in the team are not part of creating or discovering those values, they will not buy into them. Then values become theoretical and even ridiculed because of the discrepancy between them and the actual reality.

I worked with a CEO of a technology company that decided that his people would be like "Navy seals", meaning dedicated, fighting, winning. This was written on all the walls of their offices. The problem was that the organization was very average and even a bit depressed with low morale and spirit. The contradiction between the CEO's values and reality was flagrant.

Organizations and teams that have developed and agreed consciously to their set of values are faster, more collaborative and better coordinated.

To define values and drivers is a one- off process. To implement them and translate them into behaviors is a long- term journey that never stops. There are many challenges in adhering to values, including recruiting and evaluating people based on values. And more then everything, creating a culture of engagement, collaboration and inspiration.

This is where the leader's role is crucial.

For you
The leadership journey in the East is a constant conscious endeavor. It stretches from setting values together, adhering to them, translating them into daily life, keeping your team engaged and inspired by the work they do and their work together.

How you do all that is your leadership journey in the East.

To assess the level of engagement and motivation in your team, please have a look at the following diagram.

7 Levels of Engagement

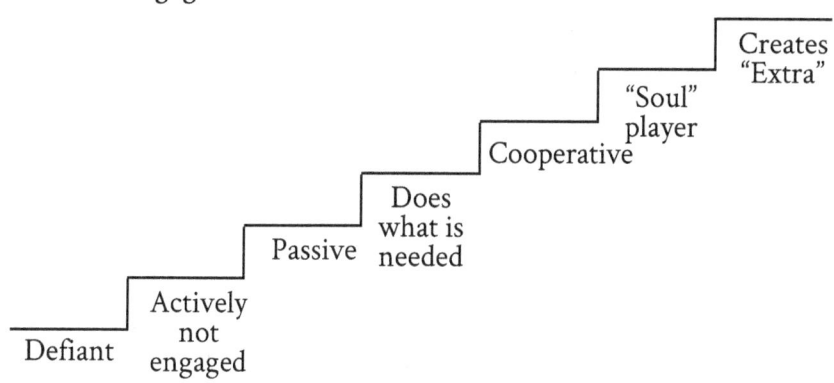

These are 7 different levels of engagement of people in teams, evident in their state of mind, feelings and actions.

For you
Where would you say most people in your team are?

Note that you can have different people at different levels, but usually most teams will be positioned inside two to three levels.

If most of your team is in the upper three levels, you are doing well. If the center of gravity is below, then you have some work to do.

Think about the people in your team from an external perspective. Think about them as human beings.

- *What is really important for them?*
- *What really motivates them in the work that they do or the added value they create?*
- *What does the work mean for them?*
- *What is common to most of them?*

Pinpoint one or two things that are important for them and for you as a leader.

Here is the work that we offer for your leadership journey in the East.

The first step to do in Team East is to identify the team's core values, prioritize and define them.

Prioritizing values is important to avoid conflict between values. As an example, a conflict between profitability and ethical business conduct is a simple one to understand.

Defining is important to understand what these values mean and to better connect to them.

Expressing values has to do with translating them into actual behaviors.

Unlike with the individual East, here agreements must be reached together as a team. It is not always easy.

Different people come from different backgrounds and have different values. Until not long ago most people worked in a family or community environment. People shared similar values and beliefs. In the new work environment, there might be people from many nationalities in the same team. It is because people come from such diverse backgrounds that this agreement on shared values is more necessary than ever before.

The N.E.W.S.® methodology is designed to enhance and look for what unifies, rather than focusing on what separates. It is my deep belief that human beings can be led to realize the common and unifying principle and progress together from there. I look forward to doing this work with larger groups of people or even nations.

For you
Try to follow these first steps of leadership in the East with your team

THE FIRST STEP IN YOUR LEADERSHIP JOURNEY IN THE EAST – DISCOVERING COMMON IMPORTANCE

I would like to offer a very valuable tool. It is called "The three circles of importance". This tool will allow you to identify a common importance that all the team shares.

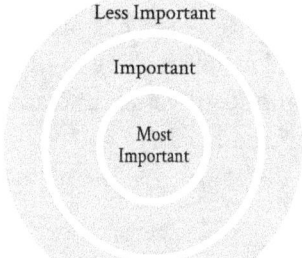

The team needs to consider this question:

What are the most important things for the group in their working together as a team?

You can use the three circles to rank their values.

You can then ask the question: "Why?" a few times to discover the deeper elements of common importance. The work is done in subgroups and then collected and discussed with the whole team to lead them to a consensus of the top 3-4 shared values.

When achieved, the team will find their core values; this is like DNA (the genetic matrix in each cell), a code that defines them as a team. (DNA is a code in the form of a helix that defines how each cell will be formed. It is unique to every individual and allows for great variance amongst people.)

A set of agreed values acts like a DNA code for a team. It defines behaviors. It defines what belongs and what does not belong. It promotes belonging and a sense of uniqueness for the team.

The level of engagement grows, and a team spirit is fostered.

For you
Care to try this with your team?

THE SECOND STEP OF YOUR LEADERSHIP JOURNEY IN THE EAST – BETTER CONNECT YOUR TEAM TO THOSE VALUES

Different people understand values differently, and for a team to have a common understanding of its core values, it is important to define their meaning together. Defining values is important so everyone understands what is meant when people refer to a particular value. Research has proven that teams with agreed values and codes are faster and more effective in their execution. Studies that compared teams with a strong set of values to teams with a weaker set of values show some interesting trends.

1. Teams with a strong set of values decide much faster.
2. They have fewer arguments and conflicts.
3. They accept and integrate or reject people much faster.

For example – "Trust" might mean in one team "relying on each other". In a different team it might mean "Giving people the benefit of the doubt" and in another team it might mean "We allow people to make mistakes without judging them". These are different definitions and they will generate different team cultures.

For most people defining values is new and many actually struggle to come up with the best definitions that they can create.

When achieved, it is a real celebration for the whole team. These values and definitions become like "a constitution" that clarifies how the team operates.

This "constitution" also reduces conflicts and misunderstandings that are widespread in many teams and particularly in management teams.

This second step is needed for deeper connection in terms of drive and energy. It is not enough for a team to know their common values. It takes deeper connection than that to establish a team's culture. Connection occurs when you define what something means for you intellectually. It can also occur when you recall the experience and the feelings that were associated with it. The connection can be enhanced emotionally by means of feelings, stories, folklore, or symbology and other methods.

The main significance here again is that the team creates the values, their meanings and the related folklore together and therefore owns it together. To make the values alive and effective, team meetings should be sometimes dedicated to case studies and stories regarding the living implementation and demonstration of such values.

For you
What are the actual meanings of your team values? Did you define them together?
Does the team actually live up to them?

The emotional connection
Eventually what really moves people are their emotions. E-motion implies the movement that can be created when people feel deeply about someone or something. It is therefore imperative that a leader in the East use emotionally connecting tools like stories, narratives, personal experiences, or folklore.

For you
- *Find a story or an example that will demonstrate to the team what is moving and important for them.*
- *Find an activity (inviting a client, visiting the production site etc.) that will connect the team to what is important for them.*
- *Think of team members who can share real-life examples of what moves them in the work they do and the added value they create.*

THE THIRD STEP IN YOUR LEADERSHIP JOURNEY IN THE EAST – BETTER EXPRESS THE AGREED VALUES AS A TEAM AND AS INDIVIDUALS

If there is no alignment between team values and the behavior of members in the team, we call it the "Be–Do" Gap: That is a gap between the East and the West, or a gap between Being and Doing.

In teams this gap is more emphasized as people mimic each other and follow the "rules of the game" that each team defines by what behaviors are acceptable or not.

Team members need to realize if there are gaps between their behavior and their stated values. These gaps need to be adjusted to reflect their values. The leader needs to look for the behaviors that will be aligned to the values that were agreed. The leader also needs to look for actual real- life behaviors that team members might have, that are not in line with these values. This is quite a challenging and important practice.

For you
How strong is the culture of your team? How engaging is it?

How aligned are the team members to the values of the team and how they operate on a daily basis?

To summarize your leadership journey in the East, please choose three situations where you personally, are going to behave according to the team values in the future.

Can you commit to your team and have them commit to each other to act by these values on a daily basis?

Can you all be open to giving and receiving feedback?

If this issue of engaging people to a team culture is important for you, here is some further depth for you to explore.

THE MEANING REVOLUTION

In 2020, we find ourselves trapped in an extreme world of hurtling technology, rising nationalism and hatred, loss of privacy, a surcharge of information and consumerism. Polarizing seems to be growing after years of hope that humanity might find a way to live in greater peace, tolerance and liberalism. The global health crisis has thrown all companies and societies into unprecedented chaos and uncertainty.

Most of the forecasts of futurists herald a world that will be split and polarized.

Physically and health-wise we will hopefully be better off in the future. However, humanly and spiritually we might be much worse than in previous years. People suffer much more fear than in the past, due to increasing uncertainty and the speed of change. People around the globe are moving toward populist leaders who promise to fix the complexity with simple measures. In a few years most people risk becoming redundant in the work marketplace.

It is time now for a new kind of leadership for teams, for organizations and even for nations.

The leadership styles and ideologies of fascism, communism and liberalism as saviors of humanity are gone now. Each in its turn.

Fascism disappeared in the 30's, communism in the 80's and liberalism in the last decade. Humanity needs a new leadership revolution to provide meaning. The Meaning Revolution is inevitable.

Meaning is the living conscious memory of your part in a greater whole. Deep meaning comes when you fulfill your potential in contributing to a larger context. The larger context can be a relationship with another person, your family, your tribe, humanity as a whole or even the universe. These are different arenas where you can find and express the meaning of your existence. The larger the arena, the deeper the meaning.

Meaning is an essential part of long-term happiness. All studies point to the combination of short-term pleasure and long-term sense of meaning as the winning formula for a happy life.

The next major story of leadership that will give renewed hope is the story of the Meaning Revolution.

To make this story real, people will have to rise above separatism and self-centeredness. They will have to search and discover their potential as a contributing part of a larger context. They will have to develop themselves and live up to it, express it and be connected to it consciously.

This possibility amongst many others gives humanity hope again. We look for leaders that will make this real.

For you
Welcome to your South leadership journey. It will require from you, strength, courage and resilience. These are three hallmarks of great leadership in the South. The mindset that is required is:

"It is my responsibility to lead my team through difficulties and limits.

YOUR LEADERSHIP JOURNEY IN THE SOUTH

The story of a medical R&D center of a large global pharma company
Our true story is about an R&D center that was purchased by one of the global giants of the pharmaceutical industry. I worked closely for a number of years with the CEO and the HR director of this center to develop this company. Most of the employees were PhDs and doctors from various scientific fields. Most of them had been working in this company for twenty years and more. They were a very talented group of people with vast experience and knowledge in their fields.

A few years after the acquisition, the CEO got a message from the parent company that they had decided to close the site down and move the activity to another country where the operation would be cheaper. The CEO of the subsidiary tried to protest but to no avail.

I was conducting an Organizational Navigation with the senior management team at the time. They were all shocked and dismayed by this fatal message. Morale was low, and people were walking around with their heads down. It was futile to explore the North with them, since they could not envision any future.

In an unusual manner we started with South work. We explored their beliefs in the face of what was coming and most of their beliefs were in the nature of:

"We are doomed",

"This is it; we have had it."

"At my age I will not find another job".

As we continued, I asked if this was the only way to view this reality. I told them how amputees can tell themselves different stories and take their life in a different direction from total misery all the way to excelling in the

Paralympic games. As we continued, some new voices were added to this morose choir.

"Maybe we should not just give up so easily. This is our life's work", and another added "Let us not just lie on our backs and give up" and then another added "Let us try to fight this decision and change it" and another "What have we got to lose? We have the "No" already. Maybe we can go for a "Yes"."

Eventually the management team decided on an alternative belief that was: "We can fight back and try to change this decision. We have nothing to lose".

The "Baby steps" were to collect a list of contacts everyone had in the HQ of the parent company and create a campaign.

We followed this with West work. They devised a plan. The plan was ingenious and very detailed:

Who will talk with whom in HQ? In what sequence?

Who will travel to the head office and with what messages? And so on. They left the room full of energy and hope.

In the following months they executed their plan. They created a "Situation Room" to manage and coordinate the campaign. I met with them quarterly to see how they were doing and add more ideas and tools. Eventually the parent company decided to delay closing down for one more year. In this year the management team worked very hard and excelled at the work they did. They created some significant breakthroughs in their research.

The shut-down was delayed for another year.

Towards the end of the second year the researchers managed to develop the next "blockbuster" drug for the entire company. Now, no one was going to close them down. Actually, a year later they were recognized as a center of excellence and the parent company decided to establish with them the global hub for developing new molecules. Then they got a very significant grant from the European Union for their research.

The R&D center exists to this day, partially due to the work on the Organizational South which we conducted together and the amazing brave breakthrough that these people achieved together.

SOUTH LEADERSHIP JOURNEY - INTRODUCTION

The work in the South with teams is as fascinating as the work with individuals. With management teams and other teams, the South is part of their culture.

In fact, for a team, their East and their South constitute its culture. The East will represent the common values and the drivers of the culture. The South will represent all the deterrents, difficulties and hesitations.

By way of analogy, the East is the motor and the South is like the brakes. One needs to release the brakes, to actually use the power of the engine and move to its destination in the North, using the road map and timetable in the West.

The organizational journey in the South has three steps:
1. The limiting story
2. The empowering story
3. The breakthrough

THE FIRST STEP IN YOUR LEADERSHIP JOURNEY IN THE SOUTH: THE LIMITING STORY

All teams have beliefs that limit their success. These come from past experience, generalizations, spreading of doubts and sometimes a true difficulty. I would like to call all those limiting beliefs "the limiting story". The reason for this is that there is "reality" and there are the stories we tell ourselves about reality. Eventually the stories and narratives of a team create the actual reality within which it operates.

The process starts by identifying the limiting belief that most team members share. Then the leader must find an "Empowering story", individually or in co-creation with the team. They need to convey it to the team, get them to agree to it, and then drive the new story until it becomes part of their mindset and paradigms.

The leadership journey in the South deals with internal and external barriers. Usually the internal barriers are derived from the perceptions of the situation and positioning in the market, or the beliefs about the situation inside the organization. They also include the perceptions of what can or cannot be achieved at a specific point in time. It depends on the attitudes of team members - whether what prevails is the creator approach or the victim approach.

The internal barriers of a team consist of limiting beliefs such as:

"We won't succeed", "We've tried that before, it won't work", "They will not give us the necessary resources" etc.

These are usually mutual stories, that people share as a team and tell themselves, which keep them in the comfort zone. These stories then create reality.

For example: A belief that our team is not appreciated by other teams and stake holders inside the organization.

External barriers – These barriers come from outside the team/organization. Eventually, as explained before, even when there is an external barrier, what rules reality is the story the team tell themselves about it.

For you
Firstly, you need to become aware of the voices in your team that might be limiting. You can hear them in team meetings, in the corridors, in the cafeteria or in written communication among team members. This is your responsibility as a leader to monitor the state of your team regularly.

The most effective way for you to discover the South of your team is to remind them of their three- year practical vision in the North. When listening to their vision, ask your team members to write down the various voices they hear in their mind, especially the skeptical and discouraging notions, beliefs and assumptions.

Then with your team, select those notions or beliefs that they personally identify with, and that they also believe are stopping the whole team. Choose the one they most identify with. This is the limiting story that inhibits your team. The South belief that we are going to address with that team. Similar situations exist now with families and communities. Most people are fearful of the pandemic. They are concerned about themselves and their loved ones. This state of concern and being a victim does not allow them to lead wisely in those times. An intensive process in the South is needed now both for leaders to lead themselves, and for them to lead others.

Best practice suggests that even if the team has several limiting stories, it is best to tackle limiting stories one by one and help the team go through each one together.

THE SECOND STEP IN YOUR LEADERSHIP JOURNEY IN THE SOUTH: THE EMPOWERING STORY

For you
When you realize the limiting story of your team, you can begin to understand its implications and where the team will end up if this limiting story prevails. To understand that you can take the limiting story of your team and "run" it through the "Diamond Model". This will allow you to see where it will eventually lead the team. Usually, people agree to change when they understand the undesirable consequences in the past, in the present and, mainly, the ones they will encounter in the future.

As with individuals, when teams become conscious of the long-term implications of their limiting stories, they are in a position to choose. Until people are conscious of having a limiting belief, they cannot choose. They simply identify with their belief as if it was the truth, the whole truth and nothing but the truth.

As with individuals, the emphasis in this realization is mainly on the future outcomes of maintaining the same perception – the worst-case scenario. This provides the foundation for a conscious choice to do what it takes to lead a change and take the creator approach instead of being a victim of circumstances.

"Empowering story" is a method of cognitive breakthrough in the South. For teams this is slightly more complex than for individuals.

The new empowering story must not be the opposite of the existing limiting story. If it is the opposite, the team's collective mind will reject it. It simply will not work.

As a leader you always need to use the "Creator" mentality at this stage and avoid the "Victim" mentality.

Then it is time to create the empowering story that will replace the limiting story and will take the team to a different and better place. It is the role of the leader to offer the empowering story or get the team to create it. The leader needs courage, perseverance and resilience to do that. The empowering story should be proactive, gradual, accepted by the collective mind of the team, invigorating and action- oriented. Many great leaders have discovered the power of an empowering story. Some examples that you may recognize:

"Yes, we can!"

"It is a challenge not a problem."

"Men who sleep in their bed now in England, will envy us the few, lucky few that fight this battle."

"This young nation can face all its enemies and win." "Others before us have accomplished such a turnaround."

"If we put all our resources together, we can go through this crisis." "They cannot break us, because we carry the truth."

"We shall never be frightened by tyrants."

"Give me a leverage point and I can move the earth." "Till the stars with the right effort."

"We can put a man on the moon and bring him back safely." "I came to help these people, not to change them."

"Where there is a will, there is a way."

"People can be so much more then they allow themselves to be."

"They can beat us and torture us, but they cannot take away our self- respect unless we give it to them".

For you
What will be your empowering story for your team? Is it Based on a creator mentality? Is it Invigorating? Is it gradual? Credible?

Can you bring it to your team?

Will it take them forward?

YOUR THIRD STEP IN THE LEADERSHIP JOURNEY IN THE SOUTH – BREAK THROUGH THE LIMITS

After creating the empowering story, it is time to break through. Breakthrough is a conscious set of courageous actions beyond current limits that will lead to a new reality and greater choice and freedom. This step requires crossing the "courage gap" which is the gap between the decision to break through in the South and actually doing it in the West. The breakthrough usually occurs with baby steps. These are practical steps that team members can put into practice immediately in light of the empowering story. These steps need to be specific actions that the team members can commit to each other to fulfill. These small steps should be outside the current comfort zone and "groundbreaking" in nature. They need to create a chain of successes in a new direction beyond the current limits. Therefore, they need to be small, practical and achievable.

For example: I worked with a team in the advertisement industry that suffered lack of trust and therefore lack of communication and transparency. This caused significant problems in performance. They decided that their empowering story would be "We can reach out to each other proactively to find out what is going on". A "baby step" for one team member was to make one phone call a week to inquire about a colleague's situation. For another team member it was to publish the main achievements of his team on the organization's intranet once a week. For other teams this might seems obvious. But, in this particular team these were breakthroughs they had never made before. The small breakthroughs brought slowly a real change in the culture of the team and it became much more cooperative.

In order to ensure that team members implement the "Baby steps", you can ask them as their leader to publicly commit to each other what they are going to do. You can ask them also to agree to be open to giving and receiving feedback on respecting their commitment. The mutual commitment improves the probability that there will be some behavioral change in the team and that its culture will evolve.

For you
What "baby steps" would you like to see in your team? How will you encourage them to take these steps?
How will you drive this and sustain the momentum?

This concludes your leadership journey in the South. It is courageous, bold and demanding. In taking this journey you will grow yourself.

YOUR LEADERSHIP JOURNEY IN THE WEST

For you
You are now invited to your leadership journey in the West. It is a focused, disciplined and practical journey.

The state of mind to adopt is "As a leader, I am responsible for focusing the actions of my team toward the required results."

Sayings in the West
"To reach your goals, you need to build a bridge between what is and what can be." Aviad Goz

"Those who do not try, never fail." Anonymous

The story of Checkmarx
Checkmarx delivers a perfect platform for DevOps and CI environments by redefining security's role in the SDLC while operating at the speed of DevOps. The fast feedback loop makes security testing of new or edited code fragments quick with speedy remediation by developers.

Checkmarx was named a Leader in Application Security Testing in Gartner's 2018 magic quadrant report. From www.checkmarx.com

Checkmarx was always a very promising company.

When I met the CEO for the first time, Checkmarx was still a small company with fewer than 100 employees. The founder and CEO started the company from scratch with a very promising vision to become the world leader in application security. Its innovation and solutions for programmers to secure the coding while writing it, were outstanding. They were going to change their industry. The company grew fast and started selling mainly to large global customers. The future looked promising. The only problem was that the company was very disorganized because of its fast growth. They had different systems which did not communicate with each other. They had a management team that did not meet and did not communicate much. Each manager was busy running their own department without much coordination with other departments. Everyone was very busy, but running in different directions. Reporting was not working well. The finance department could not create sufficient reports. Sales goals were met, but they did not have any other kind of goals. The company had a problem in their West. We conducted a first N.E.W.S.® Organizational Navigation. The results created alignment and communication in the senior leadership team. The quarterly check point meetings got off to a difficult start. At first people came unprepared or partially prepared. The process improved from meeting to meeting. There was a lot of learning. The management teams started working together.

Organizations that go through fast growth are in a very unique situation. They go through what can be called "growing pains ". The best analogy is a teenager entering a rapid physical growth phase. Their bones ache. Their ligaments stretch. They do not have good coordination. They eat a lot. They are not fully balanced.

Organizations in fast – growth phases are much like this. They are not fully balanced. Structures and processes need to change and be updated often. People who were suited to leading twenty employees may not be the right people to lead two hundred. Managers and leaders have to grow quickly or be replaced. Chaos often reigns. This was the situation in Checkmarx as well. We accompanied this fascinating process of fast growth. We worked with teams. We coached executives. We helped the on-boarding of new managers.

Checkmarx grew rapidly and slowly got organized while growing fast. This is a tremendous challenge for any company. Once a year we conducted the next Organizational Navigation process for five consecutive years.

The whole organization got more and more focused.

Yearly goals were met in different departments. Some departments that did not do well had special processes. The CEO went through each department, worked with its leaders and its people, ensuring that they updated and upgraded their part in the overall picture. This was challenging. Many people had to grow or go. So, there was a lot of human drama amidst these organizational processes.

In year four during the fourth organizational navigation process, it became clear that the whole organization was functioning much better. It sustained its fast growth and got organized along the way.

Checkmarx was now positioned for global leadership in its field. A year later the value of the company increased greatly, and it was declared a global leader in its industry by Gartner. This is an achievement that very few companies ever accomplish. In March 2020 Checkmarx was bought by an investment fund for the unbelievable amount of 1.1 Billion USD.

The work of planning and execution in the West is not always exciting. It is a disciplined, hard and long-term process of building and maintaining structures and processes that ensure success. Checkmarx, due to the commitment of its leaders, managed to develop its West till it became a global leader in its field.

YOUR LEADERSHIP JOURNEY IN THE WEST - INTRODUCTION

For you
Leadership state of mind: It is my responsibility as a leader to focus my team and lead it to achieve results.

Your leadership journey in the West is all about planning and execution. It comes to create order in complex systems. It is not simple to coordinate different departments, many teams, different systems and hundreds or thousands of people all working in different specialized fields.

There is much management work to be done in the West. We will concentrate on the leadership aspects of the West and how to develop them.

The mere fact that most people work in organizations, speaks for itself. Unless they are highly organized, synchronized and aligned, organizations do not work properly. This is much more challenging in times of change. The organization and the teams within it must be agile. They need to respond to external changes and pressures. This is even more true in times of crisis. Going through crisis successfully requires from leaders that they display an even greater capability of organizing within a chaotic scenario. They need to change structures and processes on the go and make them agile and adaptable to changes.

People come and go. Mobility grows. Information technology changes. Systems need to be updated and replaced. Digital transformation grows. Markets change, requiring quick adaptation or resulting in slow death. New roles are created to structure the organization. New departments are set up. Organizations nowadays have an Organizational Development expert in the HR departments. They have PMO's that coordinate different projects. They have organization and systems departments operated by industry management engineers.

New methods for better management are being born, ranging from TQM, to Agile, to Devops and others.

N.E.W.S.® was created specifically for this. Most team organizations that we meet are running on fast forward. They are not aligned, nor well-coordinated.

Strategy changes often but is not cascaded properly. What ensues is a chaotic movement, weak execution and poor cooperation. Almost every organization struggles with these to some extent.

In the West leadership work we help senior management teams to plan well to achieve their vision. We plan yearly goals with them. We work out quarterly and monthly plans with them. We help them to focus weekly.

Then we help them to cascade the planning and strategy throughout the organization to different teams and then to individuals. There is a difference between status or ongoing meetings and West Leadership meetings. West Leadership meetings always start by recalling the strategic North. West Leadership meetings deal with strategic focus and priorities in action. They deal with the reason for things and why we do what we do.

West Leadership meetings stimulate energy.

Then, even more importantly, we accompany their execution. We help them focus over time through endless changes, and develop the discipline needed to succeed in this process. Those who persevere, win.

Three steps in Leadership Journey in the West
Like all N.E.W.S.® directions, the West has three steps:
1. Setting critical goals.
2. Building a tactical plan.
3. Maintaining weekly focus and execution.

These are all steps for maintaing strategic focus in movement.

The daily level of activity, messages, crisis and interruptions is incredible. We can liken it to a "daily tornado".

The long- term strategy and the "daily tornado" compete for the same resources. They compete for your time and for your attention. The "daily tornado" wins in most cases. It is urgent, and noisy. It is right in front of us. It is measurable. Getting rid of it is gratifying. In many organizations, the "heroes" are the fire fighters of daily events and crisis. What happens then to the long-term strategy of the team? It dissipates, gets weaker, and eventually evaporates, and is not translated into real actions.

For you
How often has that happened to you with your team?

To keep the long- term strategy in place there are three steps to be taken.

From yearly critical goals, to monthly tactical plans to weekly focus and follow-up. They all interrelate and are interdependent.

As it is related to "How?" to achieve the long-term goals and vision, the West has a number of other elements to it.

It is about how to do things, developing skills and managing resources.

To conclude, the West is about developing effective planning and execution and having the right discipline to stay focused to achieve the desired North.

STEP ONE IN YOUR LEADERSHIP JOURNEY IN THE WEST – CRITICAL GOALS

The first step in the West has to do with a yearly focus on the most critical goals to achieve the team's vision.

Because all too often people have too many goals, the critical goals are not met. In our West journey we will start by defining the critical goals of the team.

These must be defined together; otherwise the team members will not own them. Most teams /organizations do not have this clarity and focus. They have 6-7, or even 10, different goals to achieve yearly.

Research shows that when a team has more than three critical goals a year, their execution capability is dramatically reduced. "Critical" is a perception that means, without it something will not be achieved. As an example, to fly on an international flight, one must have a passport and a ticket. They are critical for being able to fly anywhere. A suitcase and a local dictionary are quite important but definitely not critical. If critical goals are not achieved in a given time, nothing else matters.

The most important practice is that critical goals are defined by retro planning from the vision for three years forward. Basically, the question is: "what is critical to be achieved this year as a team, without which we will not make it to our practical vision three years from now? We should have very few critical goals at a time. That will help us to focus long-term in the face of the daily "tornado" and crisis. In times of crisis, it is not easy to envision a three- year vision. Yet, people need short term focus to be able to operate. It is a bit like running long- distance uphill. It is often better to look down and focus on the next few steps instead of being discouraged by looking to the distant top of the hill.

The characteristics of critical goals for a team are:

They have to be on the strategic drivers that were defined in the North.

They must be within the team's circle of influence.

They need to be feasible and attainable.

Critical goals need to be cross-team goals, so all are involved in or support their achievement. Most importantly, they need to be the most critical at this point in time.

It is easy for a leader to set the goals for their team and that is a common practice. There are usually few sources for critical goals. They can originate from the North. They can be a point along the strategic drivers that must be achieved this year.

They can originate in the East, they can be gaps in behaviors and culture to address.

They can originate in the South. They can be derived from a limit that needs to be crossed.

In most cases critical goals come from the North. Goals can be a blend of two types:

"Infrastructure" goals – These are goals that consist of creating long-term infrastructure and planning, communication and values, training, people etc. Things that will create results in the future. They are usually qualitative goals.

"Results-oriented" goals – These are goals that are associated with short-term accomplishments that can usually be measured quantitively.

Most ineffective organizations and teams focus only on short-term, results-oriented goals rather than the long-term. There needs to be the right balance between the two types of goals, long-term for the future and short-term for the imminent. By way of analogy this is like having bifocal glasses.

For goals to be effective they need to have indicators. An indicator is a measure. How will you know that the goal has been achieved?

For you
Do you have critical goals for your team?
Did you set these together with the team?
Are they measurable and realistic?
How well does your team progress towards those goals?

For infrastructure goals you need to have indicators that define the final conditions at the end of the year. Sometimes that is not a number but a binary measure – We have it or we do not have it. Here is an example: the goal is to install and operate a new ERP system throughout the organization by the end of the year. The measure will be: Yes or No. The system will either be there, fully operational, or not.

A very important last step is to nominate champions for each critical goal. They might be the champions who are assigned to the strategic drivers. A champion is like the sponsor of that goal. They are not responsible for achieving the goal alone. They are responsible to the team to ensure plans for achieving the goal are in place, and that the work to achieve it is ongoing. Champions report back to the team periodically on goal achievement. In our experience, nominating champions for critical goals is crucial for their implementation and achievement. This system alone sometimes makes all the difference. It also creates better functioning in the team with cross responsibilities and mutual assistance and cooperation.

STEP TWO IN YOUR LEADERSHIP JOURNEY IN THE WEST – TACTICAL PLANS

For you
Do you have plans for achieving the goals of your team? Are they well defined?

Tactical plans are the sequential set of activities, actions and processes that will lead to achievement of the goal.

Tactical plans can be created for different lengths of time. They can be monthly. They can be quarterly. This is narrowing down from the yearly plan. There are many ways to create a plan. For some people planning comes easily and naturally. Others struggle with it. Here is one way to create effective plans.

The "Sun Model" is a thinking model for planning and prioritizing. It helps break down critical goals into specific tasks.

For example, in the diagram above you can see a planning process for starting an on-line business. The goal is broken down into the various components that will lead to its achievement. Then the components are prioritized and are organized along a time axis.

Later, this will allow your team to categorize the various components on the outer circle into priorities.

Planning with this model makes it possible to take into account everything it takes to achieve any goal.

This is an opportunity to create long term sub-teams that will assist the champions in achieving the critical goals.

It is best for champions to prepare their plans and present them to the whole team. Since the onset of the global health crisis, critical team goals are even more necessary. They provide focus. They allow sequential activity and tracking. In short, they allow advancement in the midst of a chaotic unpredictable situation.

For you
Try to practice using the "Sun Model" and setting priorities to create a tactical plan. Please choose one of your critical goals.

Use the Sun Model by breaking it down at least two levels. Set priorities between the different components.

Create a tactical plan from these components and activities. Inscribe them in the yearly timeline.

Tactical Plan

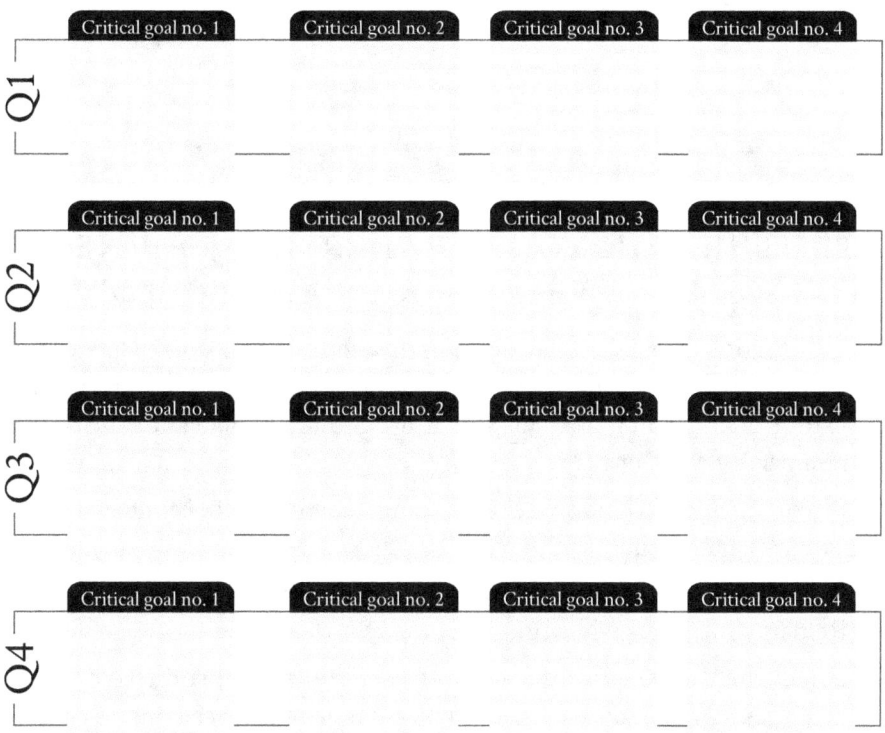

This is a table your team can use to create their yearly tactical plan. This plan will include the major quarterly activities and events that are necessary to achieve each critical goal. This table will allow tracking and follow-up by the champions and their teams during the year. These are very simple tools that anyone can operate. There are, of course, much more sophisticated applications for team management. However, they usually rely on the same set of principles that every good planning system should be run by:

1. Quarterly or monthly activities with people responsible for each activity
2. Milestones for the end of each quarter
3. Clear timelines created by the principles of retro-planning and mutual dependencies
4. Resource allocation for achieving the goals
5. Reliable tracking systems

STEP THREE IN YOUR LEADERSHIP JOURNEY IN THE WEST – WEEKLY FOCUS AND FOLLOW-UP

Weekly follow-up ensures execution of the tactical plan. Weekly planning is needed to achieve the long-term goals and vision. A week is an ideal frame of time for tracking and follow-up. It is short enough to plan and long enough to be a part of a larger plan.

It is recommended to hold a weekly planning meeting every Monday morning, together as a team, before the week begins.

There are a few steps in the weekly planning for a team:
1. Revisit your Team's North.
2. Select the 20/80 activities – These are the most productive weekly activities to move towards the achievement of goals. (See Pareto Principle).
3. Make sure the activities are entered into each team member's calendar. Clarify accountability and reporting.
4. Commit to each other to complete the activities in the coming week.

For you
Weekly plan exercise
- *Review joint organizational north.*
- *Choose the 20/80 activities.*
- *Schedule tasks for the week.*
- *Commit and account to each other.*

This is a process of a weekly planning meeting. In each area of responsibility there will be major tasks for the following week. There will be a person in charge of each responsibility, and an expected completion date. Beyond the weekly meeting there is another tracking mechanism that is critical for the success of the team:

The Quarterly Checkpoint meeting. During the year there are four quarterly checkpoints with the whole team. These meetings create a high level of accountability for the champions and the team members. The first meeting is set at the end of the navigation process.

For you
The structure of a checkpoint meeting:

Each champion presents the results and progression towards the goal that they oversaw in the last quarter. They also present challenges that they met during this time.

The team provides feedback, questions, and comments.

Each champion presents the main activities they are going to take on in the following quarter and gets the approval or suggestions of team members and of the manager. This process repeats itself every three months and it has proven over the years to be critical for the success of the whole movement of the team or the organization.

Care to try this kind of weekly meeting with your team? It is highly effective

CONCLUSION

This concludes your leadership journey in all the compass directions. The initial process is now complete.

The team has created together their compass that will allow them to navigate forward.

Their direction and their next phase are clear.

Their values are set. The behaviors that will strengthen the team's culture are agreed upon.

Their main limitation has been identified and broken through. They now have a detailed plan of how to move forward. They have champions and a tracking and follow-up process in place.

As they progress during the year, they will reach many achievements. Many things in the environment and in the organization will change and evolve.

There will come a time when it will be necessary to reset the navigation in this changing reality. The N.E.W.S.® Compass will be there when you need it.

THIS IS AN ON-GOING, NEVER- ENDING JOURNEY!

PART D - OUR N.E.W.S.® JOURNEY

INTRODUCTION

This chapter is dedicated to all our partners and friends who helped to bring the N.E.W.S.® Compass to the world. By doing this, they have enriched and assisted many people, teams and organizations.

What do we actually do and create?

I recently had an amazing experience. I delivered eight organizational navigations to eight management teams of different organizations, back to back, in the space of three months. The eight companies were from six different industries

Hospitality, Cyber, Fintech, Digital marketing, IT and Medical Production Plants.

What was unique was that for most of these companies, it was the third, fourth or even fifth consecutive year helping them navigate. We had delivered to each of these organizations the following N.E.W.S.® solutions during that period:

Annual Organizational Navigations (3-5 years). Multiple Team Navigations.

Multiple Executive- Coaching processes.

Leadership Development Programs.

Coaching or consulting to the CEO.

I had deep discussions with all of the CEOs. Together we tried to analyze what had actually happened to their companies over the past three to five years due to their work with N.E.W.S.® solutions. The similarities between them were striking.

I did not expect this. The first common impact they all described was:

We change the way people work together.

They become in fact more Collaborative, Participative, Aligned, and Engaged.

This was evident to all of these CEOs and they mentioned this as the first and most important impact of the N.E.W.S.® solutions over the years. This was on the human level.

The second common impact was that we help create great companies from the business perspective.

All these companies from very different industries had grown significantly in the years of our association.

In just a few years, the combined value of these 8 companies had grown from 300,000,000 USD to close to 4,000,000,000 USD, more than a twelvefold growth.

So, the impact was on the people and on the business, equally.

This was excellent news, as we have always looked for this meeting point between the impact on people and on business.

The most amazing feature was that some of these companies accurately reached the practical vision they had created three years earlier.

The third common impact was that:

We help create mature functional management teams.

When looking at management evolution, there are a number of things that had actually happened to all of those leadership teams. They had all moved significantly in a few aspects:

1. From silos to collaborative managements.
2. From "my own territory" to cross-organizational responsibility.
3. From random reporting meetings to on-going discussions and decision-making meetings. From slow and dispersed management to fast movement and reaction to changes. From reactive to proactive.
4. From centralized, over-burdened CEOs to actual strategic leaders of their organizations.

This significant maturing of the management teams allowed for profound development throughout these companies.

The fourth common impact was that:

We liberate individuals, team and organizations from stuck situations.

There were many issues that were resolved over those years and many "stuck situations" that were improved through working with the N.E.W.S.® methodology.

Amongst them:
- Interpersonal complexities.
- Political poorly functioning structures.
- Disagreements and misalignment of individuals and teams.
- The wrong people in the wrong "seats on the bus".
- Economic issues such as investments, cash flow and others.
- Products and offerings that were not identified clearly.
- Strategy that was not clear or did not exist at all.
- General lack of maturity.

To understand all these significant impacts on individuals, teams, and business as a whole, I asked these CEOs what makes our work with them so impactful. What those senior leaders said included elements such as:

"Your work is based on principles."

"You encourage choice, responsibility and a "driver" attitude."

"You work towards greatness and potential from the inside – out."

"You work towards collaboration and participation."

"You help people create their future together and develop shared ownership."

"You create champions for "cross" responsibility between teams."

"You work on alignment and cascading."

"You help create clarity and agreement."

"You create cultures based on real values translated into behaviors."

"You help overcome limits and encourage breakthroughs."

"You drive focus and continued perseverance."

"You actually want us to succeed and we feel it."

This was all very amazing to hear. After so many years of hard work, I felt we had achieved our ambition. When I pondered what made this possible, I realized that there were a few "secrets":

1. Strong focus on customers and their success.
   This has no substitute and is the only way to ensure success for all. Most of our partners have multiple solutions and programs for their clients. The ability to focus on N.E.W.S.® solutions while combining them with other solutions works wonders.
2. Shift of a mindset from providing "programs" to processes of long-term association and partnership. This is a movement away from the classical "training" approach to a more "consulting" approach and the drive for long-term impact. For anyone who comes from a training background, this is a deep paradigm shift. It sometimes takes a few good years to complete this transformation. Some never manage this transformation completely. When asking people in the training industry what they actually sell, the answer very often is "training days" or "programs". This approach creates a reality of "chasing" training days and trying to sell one-off programs. This is a "retail" approach, and it creates a "Vendor – Buyer" type of relationship with customers.

   The other approach, which is more process-oriented, creates a very different relationship with the customer.

   It is more a relationship of a "co-development" or "co-creation". It is much closer, more intimate and long-term. It is also much more satisfying.
3. Full range offering. To be able to accompany organizations effectively, there is a need for multiple solutions that address different needs. The ultimate situation in this approach is to become "a one-stop shop". This is a term that relates to having a variety of solutions, from OD solutions, to coaching solutions, to a variety of training solutions.
   In the words of Abraham Maslow "He who has a hammer, tends to think everything is a nail". In what we do, to assist people and organizations for long-term impact, you need a complete toolbox, and not just a hammer. Organizations are like living organisms. They grow. They shrink. They change constantly. Their needs are many and their budgets are limited. When you have a wide selection of complementary solutions, it is easy to respond to needs as they evolve.

GLOBAL EXPANSION AND NETWORK

A homage to the amazing people who took part in our journey from an Idea to Global Impact.

Growing a global network of licensees and partners is a mammoth long – term task. Especially if it is done with minimal funding. For 13 long years we grew our network one licensee, one partner at a time, until we reached a presence in 43 countries.

Of everything we had ever done, this was the most intensive on-going undertaking. We started our global journey with individual coaches in Paris, France. Our first global coach was George Stoleru, a Parisian physician, manager of a hospital. George encountered the N.E.W.S.® compass through his niece who worked with us and loved it. We were very excited by this breakthrough. We trained George extensively and very quickly he started to coach other hospital managers successfully. I remember that even while he was still being supervised as a trainee coach, his prices for coaching were outstanding. We realized that the market was willing to pay premium prices for these kinds of solutions. Soon after that was when Josie-Laure Rubinstein a successful therapist, trainer and coach joined us and adopted the N.E.W.S.® solutions almost exclusively. She stopped just about everything else she had done before. Josie-Laure was an active partner for 13 years. She delivered all our programs. She became a master trainer. She had her own network and delivered programs to multinational companies. Josie- Laure is the first person to retire from N.E.W.S.® network, at the age of 67. We just gave her an amazing retirement party at our international congress in Madrid. Josie-Laure was very well connected and soon brought in many of her friends who were professional coaches.

We conducted the first coaching certification in Paris in 2008 to a group of

20 coaches and the second certification soon after that. We then realized that the N.E.W.S.® was going to grow in the world and we opened very small headquarters in Lausanne, Switzerland. Laurent was the CEO, Odile was COO. Catherine was into content and translations. I was nominated CVO, Chief Visionary Officer, and Roni was head of coaching practices. Although some of these titles were unusual, they worked very well for us. Amongst the many coaches we certified in Paris, was Hedy Caplan, an American living in France, who was the Director of the Coaching Practice for an HR consulting firm, with a strong presence in France and the USA. We met with the top BPI executives at their luxurious offices close to the Palais Royal in Paris. After some discussions we agreed to certify the BPI coaches in the N.E.W.S.® compass.

It seemed that almost everyone who got to know the N.E.W.S.® compass fell in love with it.

We spent eight enjoyable weekends during four months in Paris training BPI. Now we were in the major leagues – training highly professional coaches with our unique coaching methodology. Our relations with BPI continued for eight years in France and in the USA. We certified their coaches, trainers and facilitators. They were very successful using the N.E.W.S.® with their clients. This made us realize that what we had was world class.

It truly is not simple to find local training and consulting companies around the globe and to attract their attention. Most have their own content that they develop and deliver. For most, the investment in new materials, localities and certification is too high.

We found some partners through our existing networks. An interesting example is Equaranda, a French group from the Rhone Alpes region. I was attending a certification of another program conducted by Pascale Demont, one of the owners of Equaranda. At the end of this certification, I told Pascale about the N.E.W.S.® compass. Then a reversal occurred, and Pascale asked to be certified as a N.E.W.S.® coach and facilitator. We still laugh about it to this day.

Another person who helped us a great deal was Ken Evert, a seasoned Australian in the training industry.

He was part of another content network that we knew and demonstrated a spirit of generosity like no other. Ken believed in abundance, in sharing.

He taught us some great lessons about giving, about not keeping things to oneself, and sharing them. He also taught us about social capital. In his mind a network of professionals could not rely only on content but must have experience at a social dimension.

Its members need to meet, to exchange, to form relationships. Ken published those ideas in his book "Designing the Networked Organization" published in 2011.

Ken was absolutely right. We adopted his ideas and started to hold yearly congresses for N.E.W.S.® practitioners and licensees from all over the world. Ken was of course our guest of honor. Over the years we held many congresses and met people all over the world, and slowly but surely the network gradually increased. Laurent was very instrumental in this.

We started the activity in Australia with the Lighthouse Group, in Thailand with Cara leading Accom, in China with Jerry and Houjun, who referred us to Clive from PLP Mexico. We went all over Europe, Central America, Latin America and Asia. This process involved endless flights, sleeping in numerous hotels, sometimes to the point of waking up in the morning and not knowing where I was.

When Roni became CEO of the company, our global growth was managed in a more professionally proactive way.

We hired a business development person and then another responsible for finding appropriate licensees and partners. Our HQ changed and evolved, bringing in experts in business development like Walter Santaliz from Puerto Rico, content development and learning experts like Galit Moskowits, and later Marina Giareni from Athens, and operations experts like Sara Marcus, designers such as Diva Moshel, and many more.

Our HQ is currently located in Switzerland, UK, Israel, Greece, and Puerto Rico. It must be said that even when global partners are found, contracted and certified, not all make it to full-scale success. The training business has many challenges. In times of crisis it is even more challenging. The training industry is always among those sectors that are badly hit. The partners need to be accompanied and coached until they make a successful entry into the market. As of this moment, it is a long- distance race. Some make it. Some drop out along the way. We have had a number of partners leave due to their inability to grow and sustain their business. Some remained friends beyond the partnership. The great majority succeeded. In our global search we met outstanding people. We found many individuals and companies who were deeply values-driven people who really wanted to create an impact in the world and make it a better place for people and organizations alike. Step by step we found stable trusted partners to deliver N.E.W.S.® programs globally. Most became friends and we celebrate our successes together.

The network that we built over the years is very unique. The partners are generous to each other. They share experience, knowledge and skill. They are open and not protective, and they cooperate gladly. I believe that creating this culture between people of many nationalities is perhaps one of our greatest achievements.

Congresses

As of the first day we started creating our network, we wanted to gather all our licensees and partners regularly to share our learning and best practices. For this purpose, we decided to organize annual congresses. The first one in 2008 was in Paris. Many independent coaches attended. It was held in a small, inexpensive hotel, in line with our financial situation at the time. Aside from content and the lectures, we had a magician perform and an amazingly happy time together.

We decided then that congresses would be a pillar in our culture. The next two congresses were also in Paris and were full of activity and fun. Each congress required very significant preparation and work beforehand. As we grew, we moved our congresses to Lausanne, Switzerland on Lake Geneva.

It is always a mix of learning, a social event and fun. Then we discovered Chateau form. This is an extraordinary hospitality chain which operates mainly in Europe. They offer access to large historical manor houses or castles, and they are specialized in hosting training activities in the most professional way. We explored their venues in a chateau in the Swiss Alps, an ancient Medici villa near Rome, a wine estate in Burgundy and a farmhouse near Madrid. These congresses added tremendously to creating a strong social network and were a powerful learning experience for all. As we are all now working remotely, we hope to meet again in our inspiring congresses in the coming future.

SPECIAL PROJECTS

Among the incredible number of coaching, navigation and training sessions, we have also had some very special projects.

Like hidden jewels in the N.E.W.S.® activities, unique needs led us to some unusual projects over the years.

Jewish Rabis as coaches for their community
The first fascinating project was to train Jewish Rabbis as coaches for religious couples in preparing for marriage. Apparently, for ultra-religious Jews, the newlyweds do not actually know each other before marriage. Nor do they receive any knowledge about sex, living as a as a couple, or managing a couple's joint life as part of their education. All rather basic for most of the readers. As a result, young couples arrive at their wedding ignorant about many fundamental issues. This results in many problematic conflicts and tragedies in the first years of marriage. A group of Rabbis decided to improve this situation. They approached N.E.W.S.® to become certified as coaches for young couples before and after the marriage ceremony. The idea was that men would coach the newlywed grooms and that women would coach the brides. The N.E.W.S.® was chosen as it is agnostic and can assist couples in building together their future life (North), establishing their common values and importance (East), overcoming disagreements and difficulties (South) and planning their life together practically (West). We certified a first group of Rabbis (men). They started to coach young grooms and the results were outstanding. Soon a second group of men was certified. One of the certifications took place in a large hall downstairs in their large central synagogue. The place was apparently double booked at the same time with another group that came to conduct a religious ceremony for a newborn baby boy. As our training was not religious, we had to give them the space.

We did not know how to continue the training, until one of the Rabbis offered the use of the living room in his apartment. I found myself leading a group of Rabbis in their customary clothing through the streets of cold snowy Jerusalem. This was surreal. We arrived in his living room, surrounded by thousands of religious books. The rest of that day we sat around the large family table and continued the training in that most unusual setting. The following morning the host called me and told me that his wife thought that the content was very interesting. "Your wife?" I wondered "but we were only men as your religion permits". He laughed and said "Yes. My wife was hiding in the kitchen next to the living room and she was listening the whole time that you were there, and she thought it was very interesting. Now she wants to learn it herself".

Jewish women rabbinates as coaches for their community

Following this success, we certified a first group of women that would coach the brides. We received very positive feedback and the certifications became regular. Young couples were now regularly going through N.E.W.S.® coaching for marriage before and after their weddings. We have managed to change the way people live together, for the better.

In France a matrimonial agency heard about this project and its success. They decided to offer a special bonus to the couples that met and married through their services. The young couples received a full N.E.W.S.® coaching process to plan their shared life as a couple. Soon after that, Israeli television invited Roni who was at the time the head of coaching practice in N.E.W.S.®, to run a TV series on how N.E.W.S.® can help couples better conduct their life together. After the series was broadcast, we got many requests from couples in distress for a N.E.W.S.® coaching process for their life as a couple.

Following this series of events, N.E.W.S.® has become known throughout the ultra-religious Jewish community and was approved by Chief Rabbis (without which you cannot really operate in that community).

The next challenge was to navigate a wealthy, extended ultra-religious family at their annual gathering at the King David Hotel in Jerusalem. The family had heard about N.E.W.S.® Navigation. They came from New York, Paris, Brussels, London and Jerusalem. The heads of the family saw that because of their geographical dispersion, the different fractions of the family no longer had the same view about where the family was heading and what was really important for them.

So, one Succoth holiday morning I found myself entering the 5- star hotel in Jerusalem. The family gathered in the big Succah of the hotel. There were about 30 adults and thanks to the authorization from the Chief Rabbis, I was also allowed to meet the women, which is not a common practice for them. We worked all that day to define the North and the East of the extended family together. The women were brilliant and helped the discussion a great deal. At the end of the day the overall direction for the family was agreed upon and so were the common values and importance. I was invited to a special festive dinner as a thank you for my services for this family.

As the N.E.W.S.® name grew in this community the next assignment was to train young Chabad messengers before they go on their mission to Jewish communities around the world. These are young people who travel the world to establish a more religious lifestyle in Jewish communities. The only problem was that these young people had no life experience whatsoever, and yet they are thrown into communities around the world to offer them leadership. The gap was incredible. We were asked to train them on how to plan their mission, conduct their work with the communities and make their mission successful. Over a period of a few years, we prepared group after group and it became a standard for preparing these young messengers.

We set up our R&D center in Israel. Israel is a global innovation center for many multinational companies. The talent in Israel offers great creativity and innovation. Therefore, many of our first pilots and new concepts were tested in the Israeli market.

Academy of high command
A whole different experience awaited us at the Academy for High Command of the Israeli army. This is, in practice, an academy to train senior army officers to become generals, much like West Point Academy for the US army. The instructors in this academy are veteran generals with extensive battle service and experience. These were people that led divisions of many thousands of soldiers in battles. They were tough, experienced and no-nonsense. The leader of the academy realized that as instructors, the veteran generals focus on the content of the training and on the tasks to be achieved and not at all on the individual trainees and their progress or challenges. As a result, the trainee generals encountered many difficulties during the

program. The solution was to train the veteran generals as N.E.W.S.® coaches. This was the the toughest ever program to deliver. The veteran generals were very closed and hostile. Every session seemed like a bloody battlefield of arguments and disagreements. At each session they had to be won over again and again. After six or seven sessions they relaxed a bit. The full program was 15 sessions long. Towards the end of the program they became open and cooperative. They had good results with their trainee coachees. We decided to celebrate the completion of the program and asked each of them to bring something that would symbolize the process they had gone through in this program. To our amazement some generals baked cakes. Others wrote poems or short prose, and some made paintings. It was really touching to hear them and to witness the transformation they had gone through. At the very end, the leader of the academy, a very high- ranking officer and a member of the chief of staff close forum, said with a huge smile and a deep sense of satisfaction, "What have you done to my generals?" Then he was all smiling and satisfied. The program proved highly useful and we delivered several more to the instructor generals over the years. The work they did with their coachees produced much better generals. As a result, it became a standard in the Israeli army that every newly appointed general would be coached into his new position by a veteran general. And so it is to this very day.

Certifying City Mayors as coaches

Another outstanding experience awaited us in the project of certifying City Mayors as N.E.W.S.® Coaches.

Newly elected city mayors came from very diverse backgrounds. Some were lawyers, some merchants, some clerks, some council members. But none of them had ever managed a complex organization like a city. Cities are much like small states. To manage a city well, the mayor needs to engage in and manage issues such as budget, welfare, sewage systems, education, construction, financial management, landscaping, crime, police, community affairs and so on. The ministry of the home office discovered something outstanding. In their first year in office new city mayors waste many millions of dollars by making poor decisions, taking uncalculated risks and making unwise investments. This costs the municipality and the country a fortune.

A new initiative was suggested. How about a process where successful veteran mayors would coach newly elected city mayors in their first year in office?

This was a great idea, except that veteran mayors had no clue how to coach anyone, let alone newly elected city mayors.

N.E.W.S.® Navigation was elected to transform them into coaches. That was easier said than done. These veteran mayors were in their fifties or sixties. Most of them were set in their ways that had served them well thus far. The first simulations of coaching conversations with newly elected city mayors seemed more like a military operational brief rather than anything anywhere close to a coaching conversation. Before giving up on them, we took a gradual approach of changing their mindsets. Practicing a new skill set. Learning the N.E.W.S.® Compass and its applications.

The meetings proceeded and a group capable of coaching slowly emerged. They became more and more enthusiastic about coaching as the last stage of their career.

At this stage it has already became clear that the last phase in any successful career could be to become a coach or a mentor to younger people in your field of expertise. Come to think of it, this was historically the way the elders contributed to the next younger generations.

After a few months of hard work and diligent practice, the first batch of city mayors was ready to be launched as coaches. They were assigned to newly elected city mayors, not in their own city. The success was immediate. The newly elected mayors were more strategic and informed. They wasted significantly less money, and their results, even in the first few months in office, were surprisingly good. Due to the success of this project, the Home Office organized a second and third program. The procedure of assigning a veteran coach to newly elected city mayors became a standard for many years to follow. Many of the mayors stayed in touch and became friends. They all confirmed greatly that the program changed their attitudes and greatly improved their communication with others.

Coaching artists for international careers

One more unique project was coaching top level artists for international careers. The Fund for Excellence in Culture and Arts was established by Rachel Marani. Our objective was to train and accompany brilliant young artists in developing international careers. These artists came from all disciplines - classical and pop music, drawing, calligraphy, dance, drumming, graphics, theater, opera, photography and more. This was a large variety of talented people, all very individualistic, though they had a few things in common, including very large egos. Most of them did not think they needed to manage their careers, but that it was the responsibility of the world to discover their talent and facilitate their way to success. This was not an easy platform for coaching them to develop international careers.

After consulting with Rachel, who was in charge of the project, we decided to start the process by working for a few days in a large group. This setting was intended to address some specific needs. The first was to create paradigm shifts necessary for them all by working as a group. The second was to allow them to know each other and to understand their common and unique challenges. These group days were very successful and produced a surprising unintentional result. Some of them collaborated to create cross-sector art projects, for example, musicians and dancers. Actors and graphic artists. In this way, innovative new projects were born.

We then began coaching the individual artists and training the project leader and her staff to become N.E.W.S.® Coaches. The individual coaching processes were challenging and fascinating. The people were all interesting, deep and complex. The main focus was to coach them to take responsibility for driving and navigating their careers. Becoming a driver of your own career is always challenging and it was even more challenging with these gifted artists. The project continued for two years.

Looking back, some eight years later, most of these artists became very well-known globally. Most of them developed international careers. The project was successful in achieving its goals.

We still meet with some of them to this day, including the lead soprano singer of the Vienna opera house, several famous classical musicians and a world-famous photographer. We also work with the amazingly gifted drummers who opened a drumming school for deprived children.

Mrs. Rachel Marani later published a book about her work with the artists, and what the impact was on her own life..

"Letting go – Love story" By Rachel Marani http://www.kinbooks.co.il/page_28647

Another major project that is happening at present is assisting businesses that were hit by the coronavirus crisis.

As we close this book, the coronavirus global health crisis is hitting the world. The world has paused. Businesses are shutting down. People are under repeated lockdowns. The global economy is struggling. In the midst of all this, we find ourselves supporting and helping our partners that are highly impacted throughout the world.

We got requests from different countries to run free webinars entitled "Navigating your organization in time of adversity". The aim was to provide thinking frameworks and practical tools to small businesses highly impacted by the situation. Every week, we run several webinars each in a different country. Each is attended by 80- 100 participants. It is both sad and exciting to share the knowledge and expertise we have accumulated over the last twenty years. There are many questions from the participants, tough questions. We try to answer.

We try to encourage people to lead themselves beyond fear towards a hopeful future. We try to help leaders to lead others in these very testing times. So far, the responses in Asia, Europe and Latin America are excellent. I truly hope that we can help these people both practically and in boosting their morale. Since the onset of the crisis our team has pulled together and worked night and day to come up with "Now, Now, Now" solutions for organizations and teams. Within two months we launched few online solutions for this time – "Renavigation in time of adversity", "Regroup and Restart"- moving from crisis to recovery, and "Advanced Virtual Leadership" for leading teams remotely. These programs are now being delivered successfully around the world. We try to add value. We try to partake in creating a new reality during this global crisis.

Like others, we do not yet know what will follow this crisis. We definitely try to play our part in helping those in need and shaping a better future for us all. We truly hope this will help.

CULTURES AND THE N.E.W.S.® COMPASS

I have been fortunate to have the opportunity of traveling around the world and conducting N.E.W.S.® workshops in different countries and different cultures. Different cultures react differently to the N.E.W.S.® Compass. I noticed certain patterns repeated again and again when working in different cultures. Some of the examples are astounding. Different cultures seem to be strong in certain directions of the compass and weaker in others. As it repeated itself time and again, I realized that it might be a cultural issue.

For example: American teams and individuals are very West oriented. They focus on practicality and direction. They prefer action and speed. "So, what do we do now?" is a question we often hear, even before clarity as to the direction to move toward in the North.

Teams and individuals from India demonstrate something quite unique. When at work, they act as if they have left their East values at home. Work is work for them. At work they are mostly disconnected from their true, deep nature. They are competitive and business oriented, while in their private lives, they are very deep, profound and even religious, with great respect for elders and family values. This inner polarity has many implications on the culture of organizations in India.

The French, on the other hand, exhibit something very different. They love to Indulge in the South. They love psychology and complexity and would stay forever in South discussions if you let them. They view Team Navigation almost as therapy rather than organizational strategic navigation. Their West and their practical inclinations are usually much weaker. They often look at the depth and complexity and are very attracted to aesthetic values, far more than practicality. In French companies, for anything to be practical it has to be defined as a "Project" and even then, it is not always practical.

Israelis are often visionary in the North beyond reasonable boundaries. They are entrepreneurial and see possibilities of doing things differently to what is usually acceptable. In the South, very often, they adopt a 'Macho' nature and mentality, to avoid revealing and to mask their fears or insecurities. Exposing these in public would be an inappropriate display of weakness. So, what you get is an image of a daring and fearless visionary, which is sometimes not entirely true.

In Lithuania, whenever work is completed and they have created a fully-fledged North, someone will always say: "But it will not happen". When this phenomenon repeated itself over and over, I researched it with different participants. "Why do you say that it will not happen if you have just created it?" What I discovered was astonishing. This nation was repeatedly conquered by other nations, Polish, Russian or German armies. As a result, they were trained over the years to believe that whatever you plan will not happen. There will always be the new conqueror who will come and destroy their plans.

Germans are very strong in the West, especially in planning and execution. However, they approach the execution phase only when the planning phase is complete and perfect. When we give German participants planning and execution exercises, they very often will use up all the time of the exercise just on planning. They delay moving into action and execution. But when they finally move, they are highly efficient and coordinated.

On the contrary, for most Central American cultures, the West – planning and execution, is weak. Even professional managers with vast experience might find disciplined planning and execution in the West quite challenging. The level of execution is usually pretty low and presents many challenges.

Many cultures such as Indian and Central American are very traditional in many ways. They tend to have a very intense cultural South as a result of their education. They have very strong traditional views of what is proper and where the limits are, often reflective of rigid internal limits. This intense South blurs their view of any possible future in the North. And so it goes on…

POSITIONING

When we started our global journey, we were positioned as a coaching company. We felt fine with that until other programs like Organizational Navigation and Team Navigation evolved. We felt that the "coaching" positioning was limiting us and all we had to offer.

After much deliberation we decided that "Navigation of people, teams and organizations" was a much better description of what we actually did.

However, no one in the training and coaching industry had ever heard of the concept of "Navigation" at that time. So, we spent some years trying to educate the market to perceive and use this concept. Now, some twelve years later, the term "Navigation" in organizations is a common 'household' word in our industry.

We are very proud to be the ones who originally introduced it.

Our positioning kept evolving. We then met SMCOV, an American firm headed by the two former leaders of Franklin Covey. In discussions with them we moved on and positioned our evolving programs to "Dynamic Navigation Solutions". Even this was still not simple enough for the market to digest and grasp what we actually do.

At this stage we already had seven different programs. We had coaching programs, training programs and facilitation programs. We were still working with marketing experts on how best to present what we do to the world. After a long creative search, we ended up with the simple idea that was to present what we offer our customers in a language they will understand. The overarching positioning was now "Navigating in Times of Change". We realized that the amount of change that companies and individuals face globally, requires better tools to navigate successfully. We divided our solutions into two main groupings: Organizational Development solutions and Leadership Development training programs.

New leadership capabilities
- Deal with the new capabilities of leading self, people and teams.
- Staying attentive, open, flexible, listening and engaging team members.

New Org. processes
- Deal with the ability of an organization to thrive in changing circumstances.
- Processes that support agility, flexibility, quick cascading and alignment.

The philosophy behind this approach of navigating in times of change was:

Constant change requires New Organizational Processes, New Leadership Capabilities, New types of Leaders, New types of Organizations. Leaders, Teams and Organizations need to learn how to thrive, not just adapt, in times of change.

The Organizational Development solutions are based on the N.E.W.S.® unique compass to create agreement, alignment, engagement and focus together with a team. These different solutions evolve from each other according to the evolving needs of an organization. Organizations go through "Organizational Navigation" processes. In changing circumstances and market situations, senior leadership team must reassess, decide and redirect the entire organization. If not, the organization can become obsolete.

They then need to cascade their compass to teams that report to senior leadership by doing "Team Navigation" processes. In a rapidly changing environment and fast organizational changes, every team needs to realign itself to the bigger picture. Failing to do so, teams will not be able to deliver the expected results. On the way, we assist their growth and development by coaching their executives. Every leader needs to develop new capabilities and be able to thrive in times of change or risk being left behind and become irrelevant.

This complete process repeats itself year after year and allows organizations to go through significant transformation. So, in essence, the OD solutions deal with new organizational processes. These processes equip organizations to thrive in changing circumstances. Those processes support agility, flexibility, quick cascading and alignment.

The Leadership Development programs are set as a three level ladder. They start with leading self with the Self Navigation program, which is the most fundamental place to start a leadership journey. We achieve this with the Self Navigation program. More and more, individuals in organizations are expected to take responsibility and drive their careers in alignment with organizational needs. Most people lack the mindset, skills and tools to do that.

The second stage in leadership development is Leading People. We achieve this with the "MAC" - Manager as Coach program. Organizations now expect their leaders to take active roles in developing, coaching, engaging and retaining their people. Most leaders are not equipped for this.

Finally, the highest level is Leading Teams or Organizations. At this level we deliver the "MAT" - Manager as a Team Navigator". In times of change there is a need to lead entire teams in a flexible, participative and agile way. Most leaders have no idea where to start with this kind of leadership style. These programs develop new leadership capabilities. They deal with the new capabilities of leading self, people and teams, staying attentive, open, flexible, listening and engaging team members.

Now, with the global health crisis, we find ourselves positioned as "Navigating in times of adversity". We did not plan for this.

It is like a natural continuation of what we have done in the last seventeen years. It seems that everything that we have been working on prepared us for this time. We receive many requests to join us and do this work of assisting teams and organizations around the globe.

The meeting point between what we are passionate about giving and what our clients are passionate about getting, moves and changes all the time. We know now that we can contribute globally.

RESEARCH

The Multi-Center Retrospective Research- A Brief Report

Some years ago, we wanted to understand the impact of N.E.W.S.® Executive Coaching and the Self Navigation program on executives and managers. We chose approximately 1000 executives and managers from 10 different countries and 12 different industries. The study over a period of 10 years, was a comparison of their assessment of the 12 box matrix solutions before and after completing the N.E.W.S.® process. Here is a short conclusive report of the outstanding results:

The Situation before the implementation of the navigation process
The current and ongoing multitude of changes being faced today, together with high levels of workforce mobility and increasing economic instability, signify trends that indubitably create a growing gap for many employees. They are less engaged, less connected to their organization's strategy for forging ahead in the marketplace, less empowered and, subsequently, often hold their organization in low esteem.

The data yielded some powerful and interesting observations on the environment that existed in the workplace before the Self-Navigation or Executive Coaching process:

- 77% of employees were not engaged with their organization and felt disconnected.
- 74% of the workforce had no vision for the future, in either their professional or personal lives.
- 73% of the teams suffered chaos. Priorities were not clear, and things of importance were not outlined.
- 80% of the organizations did not lead change and manage the development

processes, according to the employees' perspectives and expectations.
- 82% of the organizations did not perform well due to misaligned core processes and a distinct lack of synergy.

Results of a comparison between pre- navigation & post- navigation assessments
A comparison of the data gathered from the two assessments before and after the process yielded outstandingly positive results.
- 138% Improvement in clarity of personal direction and vision.
- 130% Improvement in strategic links to the organization.
- 100% Increase in team task execution.
- 90% Increase in organizational empowerment.
- 84% Increase in organizational execution.

Incredibly, the overall organizational score improved by an average of 92% above the pre-navigation assessment score, thus making a strong case for using and implementing this methodology to resolve some of the deepest issues in the workplace.

In short, it can be concluded that by coaching people to navigate themselves within organizations undergoing many changes, all individuals, teams and organizational dimensions can be improved significantly.

This outstanding evidence-based research was the first actual proof that what we have created actually works.

THE FUTURE

We are very future-oriented. My own title in the N.E.W.S.® company for many years has been CVO. This is a unique term that is an acronym of Chief Visionary Officer. Or in other words "He who is responsible to lead to the future". We know that we have created a set of solutions that most companies and organizations need. Our challenge is to access all those who need these solutions. As we develop from year to year, we access more and more organizations and create a unique impact. When we think three to five years into the future, what we see is a vibrant global network in many countries. We see the N.E.W.S.® Compass and solutions being taught in universities and in MBA programs. We see the N.E.W.S.® Compass becoming a household name in the organizational arena. Even with the current global pause due to the health crisis, we know that all this will manifest in its time.

We see more organizations undergoing a complete transformation with the N.E.W.S.® solutions.

We see ourselves much more involved in various global organizations and NGOs. Offering our solutions to resolve tensions, wars and conflicts. We see thousands of professionals contributing to their clients with the N.E.W.S.® tools. Beyond that, we would like to see that we impact a "critical mass" of people inside and outside organizations to become more values driven, more cooperative, more skilled at listening and cooperating, more participative and engaged, more caring for each other, their organization, the planet and humanity as a whole. This critical mass of people can tip the scale where the future of the human race is concerned.

OUR PARTNERS

This chapter was written by some of our partners who described their own journey with N.E.W.S. ®, its impact on them and their clients. We love to hear their voice as it is authentic and unbiased.

Thank you, friends for contributing this part.

Kirsten Watson, Managing Partner, 2_Leadership GmbH Germany
In November 2017, I flew to Prague to be certified to deliver the N.E.W.S.® Self- Navigation™ Program. Little did I know at the time just what an impact those 3 days were to have on my life and my business. When I met Roni, Aviad, Amos and the N.E.W.S.® team, I fell instantly in love. I fell in love with their generosity of spirit, and I fell in love with their sense of purpose in the world. Then I experienced the Self-Navigation™ Program for myself and my whole world began to shift. I remember feeling a kind of 'click' when I created the sentence to describe my own direction of greatness and contribution. Since then I have not looked back.

Six months later, in May 2018, we went through the Organizational Navigation™ process for what was then DOOR Deutschland GmbH. Very honestly, the business wasn't in great shape at the time and we sorely needed it. The two days with Aviad and Roni were incredible. On the one hand it was cathartic for the team, like lancing a wound, on the other hand it was deeply inspirational, and unleashed an energy, which has driven us to a much better place, where we find ourselves today. In June 2019, we held a re-navigation meeting with our new team. We were truly amazed at how much of the 2021 stakeholder visions we had described for ourselves in May 2018 had already come true just one short year later. I don't think there's any better way of explaining the impact this program can have on customers than describing what we've been through and how far we've come in such a short space of time because of it.

During all of this, I've had the pleasure to be certified to deliver all of the N.E.W.S.® solutions, which means I get to work with customers at all levels of the organizations we partner with. Regardless of whether it's a strategic workshop like Team Navigation™ or a leadership development workshop like Manager as Coach™, the impact for the participants is tangible. I regularly receive feedback about how the workshop has 'exceeded expectations', and this from people who have attended a fair number of workshops in their time! I particularly love working with Executive Coachees; it allows me to play my part in helping others to make significant personal and professional transformations. It's incredibly humbling and enriching beyond words.

So, what is it that makes the N.E.W.S.® solutions so impactful? I think there are a number of important elements. First and foremost, the fact that each solution is built around the N.E.W.S.® Compass™, which provides such a pragmatic and structured approach to work with. Secondly, working with a methodology which allows for modular programs that flow easily into each other and supports long- term partnerships with customers. And thirdly, working with the mindset that every person, every team, and every organization has their own unique potential for greatness and contribution, and that we can help them find the key to unlock it by using the N.E.W.S.® solutions.

However, and without a doubt, the biggest success factor for the N.E.W.S.® team is that they have successfully built a global network of like-minded people. People who come from a place of generosity and who genuinely believe that each one of us can be more successful if we work together and support each other. Support that extends far beyond simply sharing best practices and having the occasional meeting (even though they're a lot of fun and not to be missed!). Supporting each other in the N.E.W.S.® global network means looking for opportunities to work on projects together, looking for opportunities to help each other to grow and develop, and looking for opportunities where we can collectively bring these impactful solutions to as many people and businesses as we can to make our collective contribution.

Working in this way has taken our business to new heights and is helping us to help create Leaders who are able to navigate change much more successfully. I feel very proud and very honored to be part of the N.E.W.S.®

family, which is how I see the N.E.W.S.® global network. I love being part of a group of amazing people, who share a common vision, and who work together to play their part in bringing humanity back to the world of work.

Hywel Thomas, CEO Business fruit UK

A few years ago, soon after I met Aviad and began working with N.E.W.S.®, I had the chance to support two groups in the same overall organization who were stuck about how to work together. They both felt they had a stake in how the organization should be run but there was considerable disagreement – and some resentment – about how to prioritize, price their services and be fair in their business relationship. The dispersed global location of everyone had resulted in mainly email communication and while there was a lot of trust in that network, it meant that the collaborative spirit was steadily being eroded. I was a member of one of these groups.

So at a regional event with everyone meeting face-to-face, I took the opportunity to seek some time to run a short session, showing the N.E.W.S.® Compass and then a facilitating discussion in order to create a common understanding and build some trust as to how we would work in the future.

It worked like a dream. A few minutes to introduce the compass, and then work each direction. We start in the North, with each group explaining their thoughts and wishes for where they would like to go, and quickly we create together a shared picture of our future direction and intention for the organization. We move East and talk through our values and motivations, then South to explore our frustrations and challenges that we feel are limiting us, and our success in some way. We wrap it up in the West with some practical next steps for how we move forward.

After 45 minutes, everyone is smiling, you can feel the sense of relief. From a state of confusion and of being stuck, the N.E.W.S.® compass has enabled an easy and comfortable discussion about difficult things. We have experienced a rapid understanding and alignment of all the voices in the room about strategic and operational issues. It brings everyone together and has unlocked a renewed energy and purpose.

Peter Nankervis, CEO, Lighthouse Group Australia

N.E.W.S.® is a method and pathway to accelerate your success. It answers in a simple and effective way, the factors that need to be addressed together to achieve results, and provides an organizing system to enable change.

I liken it to the Maps on our iPhones, where we put in our destination and our current location and it shows us the quickest route to our destination. Our destination in a work sense is the Vision and Strategy of the business, where we want our teams to be, or our personal vision for where we would like to be in 5, 10 years. Our current location is where we are today, based on what is working for us, what is not working, and where we see the biggest opportunities for improvement.

How we progress from A to B is the hard part, often neglected in constant change. It starts with the reality that to achieve a different outcome you need to change behavior. The values that have led you to your current position will need to be translated differently to succeed at the next level. In a team at work, connecting to a common set of values and behaviors is what defines culture, and when done well, feels and looks like a row- boat, with everyone pulling synchronously, in the same direction.

To successfully adapt to a new plan and a new level of operating, we need to leave old mindsets and ways of operating behind and adopt new mindsets that support our new direction. This is easier said than done and why most change efforts fail. Our internal dialogue, noisily trying to protect us from failure or disappointment, needs to be seen, understood, and challenged, for us to successfully breakthrough these barriers to a new level.

Thinking without action is like rowing a boat without oars. We must translate our intentions into clear plans and action. In organizations undergoing lots of change, the urgent overrides the important, the actions overtake the priorities, the need to respond overrides the need to create. High performance is our ability to be highly productive with our time, our capability and our resources in complete alignment with what is required for success.

N.E.W.S.® provides a process and order for integrating these important factors together.

My special experiences with the solutions and programs
Every person, team and company that has experienced N.E.W.S.® has found it to be highly practical and helpful. Personally, having completed a Masters of Coaching Psychology I already knew lots of theory and evidence-based practice to help people change behavior and achieve high performance. N.E.W.S.® simplified all of this into a simple framework that connects people to business in a digestible easy way. I continue to use it personally

and as a leader in my own business.

At Lighthouse Group, we partner with businesses of all sizes that are undergoing change to achieve better business outcomes by changing behavior and capability. We have deployed N.E.W.S.® hundreds of times.

The highlights are where N.E.W.S.® has been deployed as a leadership system across all Leaders within a business. The global acquisition of Actelion by Johnson and Johnson is a real highlight.

The speed and amount of change in this acquisition really put pressure on leadership at all levels. We have utilized N.E.W.S.® as a Leadership Compass with the leadership team, then deployed it as an alignment and engagement framework within each of the functional teams. We have accredited high potentials to actively lead change using N.E.W.S.®. We have used it with all employees to empower greater ownership and accountability for leading their own change. Over three years, we have measured our progress and witnessed dramatic shifts in the Alignment, Engagement, Empowerment and Execution across all dimensions. The Sales Team itself has improved 60% on all dimensions from 2017 to 2019.

My experience with customers

We typically use N.E.W.S.® to enable strategy and accelerate the achievement of results. We primarily start with leadership teams that need to be challenged and supported to evolve to a higher level, in order to take the business to a new level.

Lighthouse utilizes N.E.W.S.® in three sectors Healthcare, Financial Services and Infrastructure. We often work with technical audiences undergoing change who have real pressure on resources, prioritization and balancing the short- and long- term success of the business.

The value of being part of a network.

As an Australian business we value being part of an International network with partners in different regions and having exclusive International IP that we can make available to our customers in a highly customized way.

It is very beneficial to be connected to a network for three reasons:
1. We can access business support by partners who can use the tools to coach Lighthouse in our growth as leaders and as a business.
2. We can access shared best practice customer applications to help improve

the customers we work with.

3. We can connect our customers who want to leverage the work to create consistency in other regions across the globe.

Lighthouse Group is an Organization Development specialist. Our promise is to accelerate the success of our customers. Having a proven pathway with N.E.W.S.® is key to our success.

Andreas Geh, Managing Partner of DOOR2Leadership GmbH, N.E.W.S.® Exclusive partner in D-A-CH Region
In the autumn of 2017, I decided to buy the exclusive rights of N.E.W.S.® for the German-speaking area. Why? I would like to highlight two aspects that today, 3 years later, fill me with great gratitude that I then followed my intuition and dared to take this step.

What motivates me is the realization that in Germany, the larger privately-owned companies are facing a major challenge. After decades of prosperity and growth, and having built successful businesses because of their very hierarchical and patriarchal character, these companies are losing their position of strength more and more in the global marketplace. The great potential that lies in engineering thinking and a very value-oriented culture is increasingly falling by the wayside because this approach simply cannot keep up with the speed of the world today. Without going into the details for why that is, it pains me to see that leaders in this new world are coming under increasing pressure and are more and more the cause of the malfunctioning in organizations, and increasingly victims of burnout and other symptoms of the overwhelm they are experiencing.

With this realization I saw the potential in N.E.W.S.® to address what is missing in this country; a leadership concept that does justice to the VUCA world but at the same time addresses the very human nature and values-orientation of our culture.

After my certification as a N.E.W.S.® Executive Coach, I very quickly had the opportunity to coach top executives with a great deal of responsibility in organizations, and was able to see how they made real breakthroughs, for instance with a greater degree of inner freedom to make decisions that have had significant impact on their organizations and themselves. Or that in difficult situations they were better able than ever to engage, motivate, and achieve shared results with their teams. There are few better things than enabling and accompanying such developmental steps.

However, what makes me personally grateful is the fact that we were able to use this approach in our own company to develop the ability for greater change and shared strength than I thought possible. In the spring of 2018, we had the opportunity to do an Organizational Navigation process for ourselves with Aviad Goz.

I am a strategist with 25 years of experience in managing change. For me it was challenging to take this step because, to be honest, I already had the impression that I understood strategy development and the ability to shape culture. So, I went into the process with a certain amount of skepticism.

To my surprise I learned that my previous approach was not so comprehensive and above all, engaging for the team. The process yielded clear results. We recorded videos about our practical vision for the year 2021 from the point of view of different stakeholders. Today, in 2019, we have just reviewed these vision videos as a team and realized with astonishment, that we have already achieved almost all of the goals we defined at that time. I have experienced in my own "body" what the N.E.W.S.® approach releases within a company and how it feels to develop my own role as a leader with this methodology.

From our own experience, we can wholeheartedly accompany companies in regaining their strength in a world of change and far beyond.

The whole world and also Germany, says that coaching is one of the most important prerequisites to successfully lead people and organizations into the future; to retain talents and to promote their potential. Reality shows, however, that it is not practical or realistic to expect managers to fulfill their demanding roles as leader and at the same time act as systemic coaches.

With the organizational coaching approach of N.E.W.S.® I realize in all of our projects, that this is no longer a conflict and executives begin to integrate real coaching in their every-day management naturally, during every employee contact. The results are amazing and encourage us afresh every week in what we do.

Marina Giareni, Managing Director and Chief Learning Officer, Greece

When something is meant to happen, it will!

We have been gratified to see and experience the positive impact of our tailor made solutions for 25 consequent years. Our latest entrepreneurial journey started in Greece, the land of gods and myths, in 2007 under the name "Learning4Life Training, Consulting & Coaching". We are a highly experienced dedicated team of Greek professionals in the Learning and Development field. We operate in more than 30 counties, in all market industries. Our mission is to empower leaders and leading organizations to expand possibilities, succeed and prosper!

We have always followed all the latest trends from prominent educational institutions, we hold highly admired professional certification, and we are capable of designing exclusive models. Due to these facts we passionately create content that meets any need, corporate culture and market sector.

This long-term practice led us to believe that partnering with any other local or global company in our industry might have few advantages to offer us. This belief actually changed during a week in Helsinki when we met N.E.W.S.® for exploratory and evaluation reasons.

I can clearly remember that cold February in the city of Helsinki where everything was whitened by generous quantities of gentle snow, the sea was frozen and the landscape was grey. The only vivid tone was the colorful furniture inside the buildings. Coming from the Mediterranean this was already a unique circumstance. The whole professional experience was balanced though, because the cold of the landscape was counterbalanced by the warm and welcoming words and attitude of the N.E.W.S.® team.

Our relationship with N.E.W.S.® was ignited in that moment, and at the time this chapter is being written it has been five years since then. This journey has actually been unfolded in four exciting and ongoing waves, that significantly changed the way we operate and brought more fulfillment to our professional and personal lives.

WAVE No.1: We realized that WE are the ones who are actually limiting the results of our company!

Thanks to our leader Aviad Goz, we were able to study his work on inner stories that really limit our results without realizing it. We hadn't realized we were operating with many restricting stories in our team's collective mind. Following the prominent N.E.W.S.® models, we managed to work on our south and overcome our main limiting factors in the years to come. This brought more confidence and stability to our company in the context of the deepest economic recession of all time for Greece since the Second World War.

Let me share with you my personal example to highlight the value we derived from N.E.W.S.®. Being in this business very consciously, from the beginning, I supposed that nothing could really stop me (us) or keep us back. After the assessment of the N.E.W.S.® methodology I discovered twenty limiting beliefs that I was personally holding. My biggest stopper was "I should not plan more business activities because this will destroy my balance between personal and professional life". This belief was preventing my company from growing further. And it was just a belief, a story in my mind! I was really happy that the moment I realized that limiting factor, I was able to create an alternative belief: "I am capable of planning some more carefully selected activities without breaking the balance in my life"! This "new story" gave us momentum and growth in the next years!

Wave No. 2: We realized that our dream network of very high quality generous professionals actually exists!
N.E.W.S.® Network is unique, generous and developmental. Our partners who have been very carefully selected by Roni Ratner, our N.E.W.S.® CEO, share common passions with us. First and foremost, we want to improve the way people and teams work together by making a long-lasting positive impact. We share the same values and this motivates us to be one global team, not only a group of companies that represent different countries and a set of solutions. Our common EAST is strong and important!

Our global congresses are priceless! They are actual experiences of personal and professional leadership development!

One example of the way we experienced this wonderful network is the fact that we won our first N.E.W.S.® deals with the help of our partners in Italy and France. They sent us the proposal templates they used at that time and despite the fact that the files were in their language, they managed to help us! They generously dedicated time, effort and talent to assist us.

Wave No. 3: We equipped our portfolio with high level, globally distinguished solutions for our customers!
The fact that we can practically improve the leadership capacity of talents,

teams and organizations is really alluring! With our N.E.W.S.® solutions our customers create their next best version from 'within'. When they conclude all their N.E.W.S.® strategic processes they plan realistically, which leadership activity they need to do, when and how! And they learn all the vital tools to implement these plans with discipline! This very clear WEST is one of the reasons we love N.E.W.S.® solutions! It helps everybody implement tactical plans and actualize strategic drivers that move the world on a personal, interpersonal and organizational level.

Before the recession, Greece used to be the cluster head for many multinationals in Europe, South Europe and EMEA regions. During the times of severe economic turbulence, many HQs had to recluster in bigger areas and the majority of Greek affiliates lost their 'local leadership'. One Fortune 500 pharmaceutical company had their Southeast Europe cluster office in Greece with no production in the country, but only a strong commercial character. The global CEO announced that Europe would be served as a whole, as one cluster, by Germany. In the face of extinction, the Greek leadership team decided to act instead of waiting for the inevitable. They had a N.E.W.S.® Organizational Navigation™ program and decided on specific plans, the realization of which enabled Greece to become the cluster head for Emerging Markets!

Wave No. 4: We appreciate the high level impact we can offer to our customers! We live and operate in an era where everything changes and the need for a growth mindset and transformation governs everyday corporate life. Strategizing for the future seems a difficult if not impossible task for most organizations, teams and individuals. The fact that N.E.W.S.® provides us with insightful processes to create a practical vision for the future that meets all major stakeholders' needs, and takes into consideration, trends and changes in the internal and external environment, is a professional luxury!
We are able to support every talented professional, leader or corporate entity to crystallize their true NORTH and face the future with confidence, creativity and determination!

From Dimitra - a middle-aged executive at a recent outplacement program who discovered her passion for entrepreneurship and aviation, to the most admired company of negotiators of a Greek global technology leader - who decided to conquer even more markets and continents, we experience the same magnificent finding: N.E.W.S.® solutions are catalysts on the journey to create the best direction and vision for the future for individuals, teams and organizations! This goes beyond the duty of learning and development; it goes into far more fulfilling waters and springs!

For us in Learning4Life the N.E.W.S.® engagement is a journey of life and friendship! It helps us live up to our name and the Socratic wisdom behind it.

We want to thank N.E.W.S.® because they support us at all times in a generous, courteous and insightful way. This is the environment that helped us grow and become a better, more successful company!

We are happy and honored to collaborate with N.E.W.S.® to such a degree that words cannot express!

Learning4Life Training, Consulting and Coaching! CREATE POSITIVE IMPACT

+30 6974 77 4000, Skype ID: marina.giareni, www.learning4life.gr

CONCLUSION

This book describes three intertwining journeys:

Your personal journey, your leadership journey and our own N.E.W.S.® journey. This book also summarizes a life-time journey for myself, and my associates. This has been a journey of creativity, contribution and leadership. We have grown from a very small beginning into a global network that influences the way people lead and navigate in many countries and countless organizations.

Most of this book was written prior to the onset of the global Covid 19 crisis. The last additions were written during this time of crisis.

This is far more than a health crisis. It is a personal, economic and societal crisis of unprecedented magnitude.

We face the break-down of structures all around.

Structures first collapse inside individuals.

Belief systems, aspirations and routines are collapsing for people. Things will never return to how they used to be. People need now to read the map often and to re-navigate in unchartered waters, and it is not simple.

Secondly, organizations and businesses need to adapt rapidly to new realities. Old ways of doing things are falling apart and new processes, roles and structures need to evolve.

Many businesses collapse along the way.

Real leadership is needed now more than ever before.

We need leaders that can navigate wisely through these troubled waters. Leaders that can take into account the human factor above and beyond the business operational factor. Both factors are challenging now.

Most leaders have never experienced this level of uncertainty, and therefore lack the resilience that is needed. It is not easy to make decisions in times like this. It is not easy to navigate yourself, your family, your team, and your organization with minimal visibility.

We try to help where we can. It is a colossal task.

Thirdly, society is changing in front of our eyes. A new generation is growing, the C- generation. They will have this crisis as part of their psyche and legacy.

No one knows where we are heading. Will humanity adapt to perpetual, on-going crisis? Will vaccines and medicines help and bring it to an end? What will humanity do afterward? Will we learn from this and stop hurtling towards self-destruction?

What other structures will collapse in the coming future? Political? Economic? Religious?

In the closing of this book I feel like a captain of a ship sailing into the unknown. Yet, I have a trust in the universe that all these changes will lead humanity into a better, more integrated and just future.

Let us sail away to where no person has travelled before, equipped with our compass, strong hearts and clear minds, with the best of intentions and the courage of hope.

www.ingramcontent.com/pod-product-compliance
Lightning Source LLC
Chambersburg PA
CBHW060827220526
45466CB00003B/1010